WALK IN SELFLESSNESS

GENESIS

A KJV VERSE-BY-VERSE STUDY

BY

LUCAS J. SHILOH, M.D

SECTION I THE CREATION

Chapter 1 The Creation of the World

Chapter 2 The Nature of God

Chapter 3 The Seventh Day

Chapter 4 The Nature of Man

Chapter 5 Man's prescribed Diet

SECTION II THE FALL OF MAN

Chapter 6 The Eden Home

Chapter 7 The Fall of Man

Chapter 8 The Plan of Redemption

Chapter 9 The Nature of Rebellion

SECTION III THE CORRUPTION OF THE EARTH

Chapter 10 The Two Seeds, Cain and Abel

Chapter 11 Dissolution of the Family Unit

Chapter 12 The Great Flood

Chapter 13 The New World

Chapter 14 Babylon and its Iconic Tower

SECTION IV ABRAHAM AND ISAAC

SECTION V JACOB AND ESAU

SECTION VI JOSEPH IN EGYPT

SECTION I
THE CREATION

CHAPTER 1
THE CREATION OF THE WORLD

"¹ In the beginning God created the heaven and the earth." Genesis 1:1

This scripture is a reminder that everything in our material world has a beginning. God alone who sits upon the throne of the universe is without beginning and without end. "¹⁰ And, Thou, Lord, in the beginning hast laid the foundation of the earth; and the heavens are the works of thine hands: ¹¹ They shall perish; but thou remainest; and they all shall wax old as doth a garment; ¹² And as a vesture shalt thou fold them up, and they shall be changed: but thou art the same, and thy years shall not fail." Hebrews 1:10-12.

The 1ˢᵗ Day
Separating Light from Darkness

"² And the earth was without form, and void; and darkness was upon the face of the deep. And the Spirit of God moved upon the face of the waters." Genesis 1:2

The creative process revealed to our human vision begins with a world without form. God however did not require matter for His creative work for He called the world into existence out of nothing, for "things which are seen were not made of things which do appear." Hebrews 11:3.

"³ And God said, Let there be light: and there was light.⁴ And God saw the light, that it was good: and God divided the light from the darkness.⁵ And God called the light Day, and the darkness he called Night. And the evening and the morning were the first day." Genesis

2

1:3-5.

On the first day God purposed there would be light, He spoke, and it was so. The sun, moon and stars were, however, not created until the fourth day. This teaches that God Himself is the source of all light, not the luminary bodies (1 Timothy 6:16). Wherever God does not exist there is only darkness and when He spoke the words "let there be light" He made His presence known in the darkness and chaos. By the introduction of His presence, light and order followed in His wake for darkness and disorder cannot exist in the presence of God.

This is true of the new birth. While the soul is separated from God in selfishness the life is in chaos. But through a knowledge of God's selfless character the darkness is dispersed, and the life becomes ordered again after the divine character. In recreating the soul that has been cast in the mold of self-serving God has achieved a greater miracle than the creation of the worlds. "[6] For God, who commanded the light to shine out of darkness, hath shined in our hearts, to give the light of the knowledge of the glory of God in the face of Jesus Christ." 1 Corinthians 4:6.

The 2nd Day

Separating the Waters

"[6] And God said, Let there be a firmament in the midst of the waters, and let it divide the waters from the waters. [7] And God made the firmament, and divided the waters which were under the firmament from the waters which were above the firmament: and it was so. [8] And God called the firmament Heaven. And the evening and the morning were the second day." Genesis 1:6-8.

3

On the second day God created a "firmament," an "expanse," or what we call sky. The waters were divided to form the atmosphere above the sky and the waters of the ocean below the sky. Without the 6-mile-wide atmosphere our planet would be lifeless like the moon. It would be extremely hot on the surfaces that are sun exposed and extremely cold on the surfaces in the shadow of the earth. The atmosphere also encapsulates the oxygen we breathe, preventing its escape into outer space. The atmosphere acts as a "greenhouse," without which no plant or animal could survive. The waters "under the firmament," or under the sky, make up our oceans and cover 70% of the earth's surface and at certain points are almost 7 miles deep.

The Savior can be recognized in all aspects of nature, as by the light so the Savior is also represented by the water. To the woman at the well Jesus presented Himself as the water of life on which she could quench her thirst. "[14] But whosoever drinketh of the water that I shall give him shall never thirst; but the water that I shall give him shall be in him a well of water springing up into everlasting life." John 4:14. Those who are weary of this selfish world will find a welcome relief from the Fountain of Life in whom there is no selfishness.

The two streams of water and blood, which flowed from the Savior's side when pierced by the spear of the Roman soldier is foretold by Zechariah, "[1] In that day there shall be a fountain opened to the house of David and to the inhabitants of Jerusalem for sin and for uncleanness." Zechariah 13:1.

From this fountain that came from the Saviors side flows the mighty river seen in Ezekiel's vision. "[8] ... These waters

4

issue out toward the east country, and go down into the desert, and go into the sea: which being brought forth into the sea, the waters shall be healed.[9] And it shall come to pass, that every thing that liveth, which moveth, whithersoever the rivers shall come, shall live: and there shall be a very great multitude of fish, because these waters shall come thither: for they shall be healed; and every thing shall live whither the river cometh.[12] And by the river upon the bank thereof, on this side and on that side, shall grow all trees for meat, whose leaf shall not fade, neither shall the fruit thereof be consumed: it shall bring forth new fruit according to his months, because their waters they issued out of the sanctuary: and the fruit thereof shall be for meat, and the leaf thereof for medicine." Ezekiel 47: 8, 9,12.

The river that flowed from the Lord's side was the river of selflessness that flows out into the desert of selfishness. Wherever the river flows it brings with it life and verdure, the trees that grow along the water's edge represent the people of God who grow in selflessness. Ezekiel's vision pictures the purity of a selfless character that will be revealed by all who follow Christ. On the selfless the promise will be fulfilled, "I will be as the dew unto Israel: he shall grow as the lily, and cast forth his roots as Lebanon." Hosea 14:5.

David describes the beauty and growth of the selfless: "[12] The righteous shall flourish like the palm tree: he shall grow like a cedar in Lebanon.[13] Those that be planted in the house of the Lord shall flourish in the courts of our God.[14] They shall still bring forth fruit in old age; they shall be fat and flourishing; [15] To shew that the Lord is upright: he is my rock, and there is no unrighteousness in him."

5

Psalm 92: 12-14.

3rd Day

Separating Waters from the Land & Vegetation

"⁹ And God said, Let the waters under the heaven be gathered together unto one place, and let the dry land appear: and it was so.¹⁰ And God called the dry land Earth; and the gathering together of the waters called he Seas: and God saw that it was good." Genesis 1: 9, 10.

The "waters" under the sky are now separated from the submerged landmasses, 57 million square miles of dry land accounting for approximately 30% of the earth's surface, emerge and rise out of the water. "¹² Who hath measured the waters in the hollow of his hand, and meted out heaven with the span, and comprehended the dust of the earth in a measure, and weighed the mountains in scales, and the hills in a balance? ²⁶ Lift up your eyes on high, and behold who hath created these things, that bringeth out their host by number: he calleth them all by names by the greatness of his might, for that he is strong in power; not one faileth." Isaiah 40:12, 26.

The solid ground on which we walk is also a reminder of the surety of God's word; "Heaven and earth shall pass away, but my words shall not pass away." Matthew 24:35. The Savior is represented as a mighty rock on which we can build a selfless character for eternity (Matthew 7:27). Self is like shifting sands, but the life built upon the rock of selflessness will endure for eternity. Hundreds of years before the birth of Christ, David pointed to Christ as "the rock that is higher than I" (Psalm 61:2), "the rock of my strength" (Psalm 62:7), "a rock of habitation" (Psalm 71:3), "rock of my refuge." (Psalm 94:22). Isaiah pointed to Christ, "...as the shadow of a great rock in a weary land." Isaiah 32:2. Self is to fall on that Rock and be broken, for those who refuse to die to self the Rock shall fall on them and grind them to powder." Matthew 21:44.

"[11] And God said, Let the earth bring forth grass, the herb yielding seed, and the fruit tree yielding fruit after his kind, whose seed is in itself, upon the earth: and it was so.[12] And the earth brought forth grass, and herb yielding seed after his kind, and the tree yielding fruit, whose seed was in itself, after his kind: and God saw that it was good.[13] And the evening and the morning were the third day." Genesis 1: 11-13.

At the command of God, the earth now brings forth various forms of grasses, grains ("herb bearing seeds,") fruits and nuts ("tree yielding seed") in anticipation for the creatures to come. There are about 320,000 known species of plants today, of which the great majority produce seeds. Green plants provide a substantial proportion of the world's oxygen and are the basis of all life on earth.

4th Day

Lights in the Firmament

"[14] And God said, Let there be lights in the firmament of the heaven to divide the day from the night; and let them be for signs, and for seasons, and for days, and years:[15] And let them be for lights in the firmament of the heaven to give light upon the earth: and it was so.[16] And God made two great lights; the greater light to rule the day, and the lesser light to rule the night: he made the stars also.[17] And God set them in the firmament of the heaven to give light upon the earth,[18] And to rule over the day and over the night, and to divide the light from the darkness: and God saw that it was good.[19] And the evening and the morning were the fourth day." **Genesis 1:14-19.**

The sun, "the greater light," which is the center of our solar system is 109 times bigger than the Earth and comprises 99% of the total mass of our solar system. Every second, the sun's core fuses over 600 million tons of hydrogen into helium, and in the process converts 4 million tons of matter into energy. The temperature of the sun at its core is roughly 27 million degrees Fahrenheit. Every 1.5 millionths of a second, the sun releases more energy than all humans consume in an entire year.

The average distance of the earth from the sun is 92 million miles, it takes 365 and a 1/4 days for the earth to orbit the sun thus providing us with our yearly cycle. The earth travels at a speed of approximately 66,000 miles per hour and covers 585 million miles per year.

The moon, "the lesser light," orbits the earth every 29.5 days and provides us with our monthly cycle. The earth rotates at an approximate 1000 miles per hour on its own axis completing one revolution in 24 hours thus providing us with our day and night cycles. The tilt of the earth's axis in its elliptical orbit around the sun provides us with the four seasons, all the while the night skies are lit with over 200 billion trillion stars.

These luminary bodies are also a faint representation of our Savior. Christ is the "Sun of Righteousness," or the "Sun of Selflessness." As the sun brings light and life to our solar system so the "Sun of Righteousness" brings life and healing to the soul lost in the service of self. "2 But unto you that fear my name shall the Sun of righteousness arise with healing in his wings; and ye shall go forth, and grow up as calves of the stall." Malachi 4:2. Christ is also represented by the "day star" or the "morning star," which is the last star in the sky as the sun begins to rise, guiding the selfish into the glorious light of day. "16 ...I am the root and the offspring of David, and the bright and morning star." Revelation 22: 16."19...until the day dawn, and the day star arise in your hearts." 2 Peter 1: 19.

Before the birth of Christ, it was prophesied of Him, "2 The people that walked in darkness have seen a great light: they that dwell in the land of the shadow of death, upon them hath the light shined." Isaiah 9:2. "12 Then spake Jesus again unto them, saying, I am the light of the world: he that followeth me shall not walk in darkness, but shall have the light of life." John 8:12. Those that follow the Savior in the path of self-sacrifice walk in the light. "18 But the path of the just is as the shining light, that shineth more and more unto the perfect day.19 The way of the wicked is as darkness: they know not at what they stumble." Proverbs 4:18,19.

5th Day

Creatures of the Sea and Air

"20 And God said, Let the waters bring forth abundantly the moving creature that hath life, and fowl that may fly above the earth in the open firmament of heaven.21 And God created great whales, and every living creature that moveth, which the waters brought forth abundantly, after their kind, and every winged fowl after his kind: and God saw that it was good.22 And God blessed them, saying, Be fruitful, and multiply, and fill the waters in the seas, and let fowl multiply in the

9

earth.[23] And the evening and the morning were the fifth day." Genesis 1:20-23.

On the 5th day God now speaks the word and the air is filled instantly with more than 11,000 known species of birds and the oceans are instantly populated by over 33,000 species of fish. God blessed them to be fruitful and today there are an estimated 50 billion birds globally and 3.5 trillion fish in the ocean.

6th Day

Land-Based Animals, Man & their Diet.

"[24] And God said, Let the earth bring forth the living creature after his kind, cattle, and creeping thing, and beast of the earth after his kind: and it was so.[25] And God made the beast of the earth after his kind, and cattle after their kind, and every thing that creepeth upon the earth after his kind: and God saw that it was good." Genesis 1:24, 25.

On the 6th day God spoke the word and the landmasses became instantly populated with a variety of creatures. There are over 1.7 million species of animals and close to a million insect species that inhabit the earth.

"[26] And God said, Let us make man in our image, after our likeness: and let them have dominion over the fish of the sea, and over the fowl of the air, and over the cattle, and over all the earth, and over every creeping thing that creepeth upon the earth. [27] So God created man in his own image, in the image of God created he him; male and female created he them." Genesis 1:26, 27.

The crowning act of creation was the bringing forth of mankind created in the selfless image of God. Genesis Chapter 2 describes the creation of mankind in more detail.

"[28] And God blessed them, and God said unto them, Be fruitful, and multiply, and replenish the earth, and subdue it: and have dominion over the fish of the sea, and over the fowl of the air, and over every living thing that moveth upon the earth" Genesis 1:28.

The earth was to be man's home, he was to maintain it and care for its creatures. In this simple scripture man's responsibility to the animal kingdom is presented. While God held title to the earth; man was to be its keeper.

"**29 And God said, Behold, I have given you every herb bearing seed, which is upon the face of all the earth, and every tree, in the which is the fruit of a tree yielding seed; to you it shall be for meat.30 And to every beast of the earth, and to every fowl of the air, and to every thing that creepeth upon the earth, wherein there is life, I have given every green herb for meat: and it was so.31 And God saw every thing that he had made, and, behold, it was very good. And the evening and the morning were the sixth day." Genesis 1:29-31.**

In a world without selfishness and its inevitable consequences of death God gave both man and beast a plant-based diet: grains ("herb bearing seed"), fruits and nuts ("fruit of a tree yielding seed"). The marvelous creative process ends at the end of the 6th day in Genesis Chapter one. Genesis Chapter two brings to view the close of the creative week with the seventh day of rest as well as additional details on the creation of man.

CHAPTER 2

THE NATURE OF GOD

The Godhead

"[26] And God said, Let us make man in our image, after our likeness…" Genesis 1:26

The plural "us" is a reference to the three members of the "Godhead" (Romans 1:20), which includes God the Father, God the Son and God the Holy Spirit. These three have existed through all eternity, one in character and purpose but three separate entities. "[7] For there are three that bear record in heaven, the Father, the Word, and the Holy Ghost: and these three are one." 1 John 5:7. In the beginning the Father conceived the plan and design of creation, Christ spoke the words for He is the "Word of God" (John 1:1) and the Holy Spirit executed the command by moving over the face of the waters.

Before coming to this earth Christ had existed as co-creator with the Father from all eternity. Christ is not a created being but like the Father is pre-existent, self-existent with life that is un-derived. "[1] In the beginning was the Word, and the Word was with God, and the Word was God.[2] The same was in the beginning with God.[3] All things were made by him; and without him was not any thing made that was made." John 1:1-3.

"[8] But unto the Son he saith, Thy throne, O God, is for ever and ever: a sceptre of righteousness is the sceptre of thy kingdom." Hebrews 1:8. "[16] For by him were all things created, that are in heaven, and that are in earth, visible and invisible, whether they be thrones, or dominions, or principalities, or powers: all things were created by him, and for him:[17] And he is before all things, and by him all things consist." Colossians 1:16,17.

Christ "the Word," the second member of the Godhead came to this earth in human form. "[23] Behold, a virgin shall be with child, and shall bring forth a son, and they shall call his name Emmanuel, which being interpreted is, God with us." Matthew 1:23. "The Word was made flesh, and dwelt among us." (John 1:14). "Lo, I come... Sacrifice and offering Thou wouldest not, but a body hast Thou prepared Me.... Lo, I come (in the volume of the Book it is written of Me,) to do Thy will, O God." Hebrews 10:5-7.

The purpose of the incarnation was three-fold: to atone for man's sin, to demonstrate that when humanity was united with divinity that man could live a holy or selfless life and to reveal the character of the Father before the universe, "...he that hath seen me hath seen the Father." John 14:9. The entire life of Christ from the manger to the cross reflected the Father's selfless character. "Who being the brightness of his glory, and the express image of his person..." Hebrews 1:3.

Through the virgin birth, Christ received His physical body from His mother and His selfless character from His Heavenly Father. Thus, He was the Son of Man (Mark 14:62) and the Son of God (Mark 1:11). "[14] As the children are partakers of flesh and blood, he also himself likewise took part of the same." Hebrews 2:14. Walking amongst men Jesus was completely human and yet completely divine. As Christ walked the earth, He was tired, cold and hungry and when He performed miracles or calmed the ocean He did so through faith in His Father, not by His own divinity. "[19]...The Son can do nothing of himself, but what he seeth the Father do: for what things soever he doeth, these

14

also doeth the Son likewise." John 5:19. "He was tempted in all points as we are yet without sin." Hebrews 4:15. Christ could have sinned but did not, he did not use His divinity to escape temptation or lighten his work for then He would not be our perfect example. Through the blend of divinity and humanity within Himself Christ demonstrated that when man unites with God, he can live a selfless life.

God the Father

"[1] In the beginning __God__ ("Elohim") created the heaven and the earth." Genesis 1:1

The word "God" in the King James Version is translated from the Hebrew word "Elohim" and represents the Godhead as a whole: God the Father, God the Son and God the Holy Spirit. Thus, in Genesis 1:1 we see all three members of the Godhead working together in creating the world.

"[7] And the L<small>ORD</small> __God__ ("Yahweh Elohim") formed man of the dust of the ground…" Genesis 2:7.

In the King James Version, the word "LORD" in capital letters as demonstrated in the above scripture is translated from the Hebrew "YHWH" pronounced YAHWEH which is the personal name of the Father and in English is translated as "Jehovah." Thus, in Genesis 2:7 we see the specific action of "YAHWEH Elohim," the Father Himself, forming man out of the dust of the ground. Throughout the King James Version the word "LORD" in capital letters always refers to the Father by His actual name, YAHWEH. The word "lord" in small letters is translated from the Hebrew word "adonai" which means "master," a term of respect.

God the Son

"[1]Now Moses kept the flock of Jethro his father in law….[2] And the __angel of the L__<small>ORD</small> ("malak YAHWEH") appeared unto him in a flame of fire out of the midst of a bush… [6] Moreover he said, I am the God ("Elohim") of thy father, …. [14] And God ("Elohim") said unto Moses, I A<small>M</small> T<small>HAT</small> I A<small>M</small>: and he said, Thus shalt thou say

16

unto the children of Israel, I AM hath sent me unto you...." Exodus 3: 1,2,6,14.

In this scripture the "angel of the LORD" appears to Moses. The word "angel" in Hebrew is "malak," which means "messenger" and "malak YAHWEH" simply means the "messenger of the LORD." This is however no ordinary angel for He claims to Himself the title of God and the title of the Great I AM. This angel or messenger is none other the Christ Himself, the "WORD," for He bears the messages from the Father to mankind, for the "Word was with God, and the Word was God." John 1:1. Throughout the Old Testament Christ is revealed as "the angel of the LORD."

"[56] Your father Abraham rejoiced to see my day: and he saw it, and was glad.[57] Then said the Jews unto him, Thou art not yet fifty years old, and hast thou seen Abraham? [58]Verily, verily, I say unto you, Before Abraham was, I am." John 8:56-58. Jesus is the "I AM" for He is all and in all for His people, "I am the Good Shepherd." "I am the living Bread." "I am the Way, the Truth, and the Life." John 10:11; 6:51; 14:6.

It was Christ himself who led the people out of Egypt opening their way through the Red Sea. "[20] Behold, I send an Angel before thee, to keep thee in the way, and to bring thee into the place which I have prepared. [21] Beware of him, and obey his voice, provoke him not; for he will not pardon your transgressions: for my name is in him.[22] But if thou shalt indeed obey his voice, and do all that I speak; then I will be an enemy unto thine enemies, and an adversary unto thine adversaries" Exodus 23:20-22. "[1] Moreover, brethren, I would not that ye should be ignorant, how that all our fathers were under the cloud, and all passed through the sea;

² And were all baptized unto Moses in the cloud and in the sea; ³ And did all eat the same spiritual meat; ⁴ And did all drink the same spiritual drink: for they drank of that spiritual Rock that followed them: and that Rock was Christ." 1 Corinthians 10:1-4.

The Incarnation of Christ

The incarnation of Christ is a mystery; "⁶ Who, being in the form of God, thought it not robbery to be equal with God:⁷ But made himself of no reputation, and took upon him the form of a servant, and was made in the likeness of men:⁸ And being found in fashion as a man, he humbled himself, and became obedient unto death, even the death of the cross." Philippians 2: -11.

Christ thought it not "robbery to be equal with God," that is Christ was not content to be God while man was lost. Christ gave the scepter back into the Father's hand, stepped down from the throne of the universe, took on human flesh and came to this world as a man. As a child Christ received religious instruction at His mother's knee listening to the very words, He Himself had spoken to Moses and the prophets. He possessed all the resources of the universe, yet He lived the life of a poor man and while dying the death of a criminal He grants eternal life to the thief beside him. These are the marvelous contradictions of the incarnation that meet at the Cross of Calvary.

God the Holy Spirit

"…And the Spirit ("Ruach") of God moved upon the face of the waters." Genesis 1:2

Here we are introduced to the third member of the

Godhead, God the Holy Spirit as He hovers over the face of the waters waiting to execute the divine command and bring the world into material existence. The Holy Spirit is the "Spirit of Holiness" for all who come under His influence are made holy or selfless. The same creative power that the Holy Spirit used to bring the world into material existence is used to transform the character from selfish to selfless in the process known as "sanctification" (1 Corinthians 6:11).

No man can change the selfish character of himself, "[23] Can the Ethiopian change his skin or the leopard his spots? Then also you can do good who are accustomed to do evil." Jeremiah 13:23. But through the Holy Spirit this change is made: "[26] A new heart also will I give you, and a new spirit will I put within you: and I will take away the stony heart out of your flesh, and I will give you an heart of flesh. [27] And I will put my spirit within you, and cause you to walk in my statutes, and ye shall keep my judgments, and do them." Ezekiel 36:26-27.

The three members of the Godhead have worked together in the creation of the world and the re-creation of the soul that has been ruined by selfishness. In the beginning the Father conceived the plan and design of creation, Christ spoke the words for He is the "Word of God" (John 1:1) and the Holy Spirit executed the command by moving over the face of the waters.

In the plan of salvation, the Father conceived of the plan to redeem man, Christ provided the sacrifice to justify the guilty sinner and the Holy Spirit transforms the character into selflessness thus bringing man back to peace with the Father. Without this transformation of character, no man shall see the kingdom of heaven, for selflessness is the foundation of God's character and the Rule of Law that governs the universe at large.

CHAPTER 3
THE SEVENTH DAY
The Purpose of the Sabbath

"[1]Thus the heavens and the earth were finished, and all the host of them.[2] And on the seventh day God ended his work which he had made; and he rested on the seventh day from all his work which he had made.[3] And God blessed the seventh day, and sanctified it: because that in it he had rested from all his work which God created and made.[4] These are the generations of the heavens and of the earth when they were created, in the day that the LORD God made the earth and the heavens." Genesis 2:1-4.

At the end of creation God "rested" from His work. The word "rested" is from the Hebrew word "Sabbath" which means to "cease" from labor. God's rest was in no wise from exhaustion "[28] Hast thou not known? hast thou not heard, that the everlasting God, the LORD, the Creator of the ends of the earth, fainteth not, neither is weary?..." Isaiah 40:28.

God had created the world in selflessness; His sole purpose of creation was to bring joy to those whom He created. God both "blessed" and "sanctified" the seventh day as a monument of creation; it was given as a blessing, and as such a day of enjoyment. He also sanctified the day thus setting it aside for religious instruction by which we might grow in selfless perfection.

"[8] Remember the sabbath day, to keep it holy.[9] Six days shalt thou labour, and do all thy work: [10] But the seventh day is the sabbath of the LORD thy God: in it thou shalt not do any work, thou, nor thy son, nor thy daughter, thy manservant, nor thy maidservant, nor thy cattle, nor thy stranger that is within thy gates:[11] For in six days the LORD made heaven and earth, the sea, and all that in them is, and rested the seventh day: wherefore the LORD blessed the sabbath day, and hallowed it." Genesis 20:8-11.

The great Principle of Selflessness by which the universe is governed is exhaustless and the Ten Commandments (Exodus 20:8-11) is an abbreviated form of this exhaustless principle. The commandments are framed as a caution against self-serving and its inevitable consequences of harm; "Thou shalt not be self-serving and cause harm by stealing, killing etc…"

The fourth commandment of the sabbath calls for rest thus preventing harm to both the human machinery and the social relationships of the nuclear family unit. It's a time for family cohesion and for religious instruction. By Jewish tradition the day before the Sabbath was termed the "preparation day" (Mark 15:42; Luke 23:54; John 19:31) by which families cooked, cleaned, and prepared their homes before opening the Sabbath in song and prayer.

Timing of the Sabbath

"…And the evening and the morning were the sixth day." Genesis 1:31

Each of the six creative days ends with the phrase "the evening and the morning" were the first day, the second day etc. indicating that each day begins with rest starting at sunset. Under Emperor Julius Ceasar the format of a day was changed from the biblical "sunset to sunset" to the pagan form of "midnight to midnight." Friday, the 6th day of the week ends at sunset at which time the evening of the 7th day commences lasting till Saturday sunset, at which time the evening of the first day of the week begins. Thus, the Sabbath of God is observed Friday sunset to Saturday sunset and not midnight to midnight according to our modern-day calendar.

The Sabbath was "transferred" from Saturday to Sunday when Roman Emperor Constantine converted to Christianity and legalized Sunday worship in the enforcement law of March 7, A.D. 321: "On the venerable Day of the Sun let the magistrates and people residing in cities rest, and let all workshops be closed." (Codex Justinianus 3.12.3, trans. Philip Schaff, History of the Christian Church, 5th ed. (New York, 1902), 3:380, note 1.)

At the Church Council of Laodicea in AD 364 the Christian church coded Constantine's Sunday decree into church doctrine and changed the name of the "sabbath" to the "Lord's day:" "Christians shall not Judaize and be idle on Saturday but shall work on that day; but the Lord's Day they shall especially honour, and, as being Christians, shall, if possible, do no work on that day. If, however, they are found Judaizing, they shall be shut out from Christ" (Strand, op. cit., citing Charles J. Hefele, A History of the Councils of the Church, 2 [Edinburgh, 1876] 316).

The Savior however has cautioned on adopting human traditions; "9 But in vain they do worship me, teaching for doctrines the commandments of men." Mathew 15:9. Observance of the first day of the week as designated by a self-serving man, would naturally fail to be the appropriate symbol of selflessness.

23

The Sabbath and the Crucifixion Week

"**[31]** **The Jews therefore, because it was the preparation, that the bodies should not remain upon the cross on the sabbath day, (for that sabbath day was an high day,) besought Pilate that their legs might be broken, and that they might be taken away.[32] Then came the soldiers, and brake the legs of the first, and of the other which was crucified with him.[33] But when they came to Jesus, and saw that he was dead already, they brake not his legs:" John 19:31-33…. "In the end of the sabbath, as it began to dawn toward the first day of the week, came Mary Magdalene and the other Mary to see the sepulchre." Mathew 28:1**

The creative week is closely associated with the plan of salvation, as seen in the closing scenes of the life of Christ. Christ died late on Friday afternoon (the 6th day), He rested in the tomb on Saturday (the 7th day) and rose on Sunday (the 1st day). Christ's work in redeeming man ended with a Sabbath of rest just as He did at the close of creation. The creation of the world and the re-creation of the human nature ruined by selfishness are both commemorated by Christ Himself with a day of rest, as both events were conceived and executed in selflessness. The number 7 in Bible numerology indicates completion.

The Sabbath in the Time of Christ

"**[23] And it came to pass, …went through the corn fields on the sabbath day; and his disciples began, as they went, to pluck the ears of corn.[24] And the Pharisees said unto him, Behold, why do they on the sabbath day that**

24

which is not lawful?²⁵ And he said unto them, Have ye never read what David did, when he had need, and was an hungred, he, and they that were with him?²⁶ How he went into the house of God in the days of Abiathar the high priest, and did eat the shewbread, which is not lawful to eat but for the priests, and gave also to them which were with him?²⁷ And he said unto them, The sabbath was made for man, and not man for the sabbath:²⁸ Therefore the Son of man is Lord also of the sabbath." Mark 2:23-28

In the time of Christ, the true meaning of the sabbath as a day of family enjoyment and religious instruction was lost sight of and the caviling Jews had become slaves to rabbinical traditions. Today turning on a light switch is considered a violation of the sabbath according to Orthodox Jews, as this constitutes work. These traditions made the sabbath a loathsome burden and Christ swept away these erroneous conceptions citing his authority as the Lord of the Sabbath for He was co-creator with the Father (Colossians 1:16). Christ came to "magnify the law, and make it honourable." Isaiah 42:2.

"¹⁶ Let no man therefore judge you in meat, or in drink, or in respect of an holyday, or of the new moon, or of the sabbath days: ¹⁷ Which are a shadow of things to come; but the body is of Christ." Colossians 2:16, 17. "⁹ But now, after that ye have known God, or rather are known of God, how turn ye again to the weak and beggarly elements, whereunto ye desire again to be in bondage? ¹⁰ Ye observe days, and months, and times, and years." Galatians 4:10.

Through the centuries the Jews came to view ritual

observance as a means of "earning" salvation and the apostle Paul spent much time correcting this error in his letters to Colossus and Galatia. In these scriptures Paul states that no amount of ritual will save a person, only the sacrifice of Christ. Our title to heaven is as it was in Eden, the free gift of a selfless character; a character that is a full reflection of that great Principle of Selflessness. The ritual of Sabbath observance when it is used for rest, family cohesion and religious instruction facilitates the purification of the character, apart from this there is no merit in mere Sabbath observance.

"[12] Moreover also I gave them my sabbaths, to be a sign between me and them, that they might know that I am the LORD that sanctify them." Ezekiel 20:12.

Sabbath observance is a joyful acknowledgment of God's ownership over us and it will remain for all time as a day of family cohesion, instruction and growth: "[22] For as the new heavens and the new earth, which I will make, shall remain before me, saith the LORD, so shall your seed and your name remain.[23] And it shall come to pass, that from one new moon to another, and from one sabbath to another, shall all flesh come to worship before me, saith the LORD." Isaiah 66:22, 23.

CHAPTER 4

THE NATURE OF MAN

The Creation of Man

"⁷ And the LORD God formed man of the dust of the ground, and breathed into his nostrils the breath ("neshamah") of life; and man became a living soul ("nephesh")." Genesis 2:7

God the Father Himself now breathes a "breath" of life into the lifeless form of Adam who then becomes a "living soul." The word "breath" is from the Hebrew word "neshamah" which simply means "breath;" if it were a spirit entity then the Hebrew would read "ruach." This "neshamah" or breath of life is also used elsewhere in scripture in relation to animals and the breath of life within them. (Genesis 7:2)

The scripture states that man became a "living soul," a translation from the Hebrew word "nephesh" which is translated elsewhere in the King James Version as: "life" (1 Kings 17:21), "heart" (Genesis 34:3), "living being" (Genesis 12:5) and "person" (Numbers 31:19). The New King James Version correctly renders "nephesh" in Genesis 2:7 as a "living being." The notion of a mystical immortal entity termed "soul" has its roots in ancient paganism. God alone who sits on the throne of the universe is without beginning and without end (1 Timothy 6:16).

"⁴ His breath goeth forth, he returneth to his earth; in that very day his thoughts perish." Psalms 146:4. "⁵ For the living know that they shall die: but the dead know not any thing, neither have they any more a

27

reward; for the memory of them is forgotten. **⁶ Also their love, and their hatred, and their envy, is now perished; neither have they any more a portion for ever in any thing that is done under the sun." Ecclesiastes 9: 5, 6.**

When man dies the "breath," the "neshamah," returns to God and man returns to the dust from which he was taken. At that very moment man ceases to exist for all his thoughts and feelings disappear, as these are the products of the brain, - not an immortal spirit entity.

"¹² So man lieth down, and riseth not: till the heavens be no more, they shall not awake, nor be raised out of their sleep..." Job 14: 12. "¹⁶ For the Lord himself shall descend from heaven with a shout, with the voice of the archangel, and with the trump of God: and the dead in Christ shall rise first: ¹⁷ Then we which are alive and remain shall be caught up together with them in the clouds, to meet the Lord in the air: and so shall we ever be with the Lord.¹⁸ Wherefore comfort one another with these words." 1 Thessalonians 4:16-18."²⁹ Men and brethren, let me freely speak unto you of the patriarch David, is both dead and buried, and his sepulcher is with us unto this day...³⁴ For David is not ascended into the heavens." Acts 2:29, 34.

The righteous dead remain in their graves asleep. At Christ's return He will call them forth to eternal life.

Ancient Myths and Pagan Christianity

The ancient Greeks believed in Hades, the god of the underworld. Hades was the brother to the Olympian god Zeus. According to myth, at death a person's essence or soul was separated from the corpse and ferried by Charon to the underworld via several rivers.

The first was the river Styx which circled the underworld seven times thus separating the souls from the land of the living. Next these souls were to drink from the river Lethe, the river of oblivion so that the souls would forget their earthly existence. Once their memories were wiped clean the souls would travel along the River Phlegethon, the River of Fire, where they were judged and incarcerated in the prison of the Titans.

The prison cells were conceptualized as a labyrinth at the center of the earth consisting of dark, cold, and joyless halls. Throughout the Classical (500–323 BCE) and Hellenistic (323–30 BCE) periods and during the long span of the Roman Empire, these teachings of the underworld became increasingly "infernalized" which was subsequently adopted into pagan Christianity.

In the Old Testament the Hebrew word "sheol" is translated 65 times as "hell," 31 times as "the grave" and 3 times as the "pit." In the Greek New Testament, the equivalent word for "sheol" is "hades" and is found a total of 11 times, 10 being translated as "hell" and one time as the "grave." The Hebrew "Sheol," the Greek "hades," "the pit" or "hell" is nothing more than the grave, a state of non-existence.

Misunderstood Bible Verses on Man's Mortality

"[19] There was a certain rich man, which was clothed in purple and fine linen, and fared sumptuously every day:[20] And there was a certain beggar named Lazarus, which was laid at his gate, full of sores,[21] And desiring to be fed with the crumbs which fell from the rich man's table: moreover the dogs came and licked his sores.

[22] And it came to pass, that the beggar died, and was carried by the angels into Abraham's bosom: the rich man also died, and was buried;[23] And in hell he lift up his eyes, being in torments, and seeth Abraham afar off, and Lazarus in his bosom.[24] And he cried and said, Father Abraham, have mercy on me, and send Lazarus, that he may dip the tip of his finger in water, and cool my tongue; for I am tormented in this flame.

[25] But Abraham said, Son, remember that thou in thy lifetime receivedst thy good things, and likewise Lazarus evil things: but now he is comforted, and thou art tormented.[26] And beside all this, between us and you there is a great gulf fixed: so that they which would pass from hence to you cannot; neither can they pass to us, that would come from thence.

[27] Then he said, I pray thee therefore, father, that thou wouldest send him to my father's house:[28] For I have five brethren; that he may testify unto them, lest they also come into this place of torment.[29] Abraham saith unto him, They have Moses and the prophets; let them hear them.[30] And he said, Nay, father Abraham: but if one went unto them from the dead, they will repent.[31] And he said unto him, If they hear not Moses and the prophets, neither will they be persuaded, though one rose from the dead." Luke 16:19-31.

In this parable Christ used the pagan belief system of the day to teach several important lessons through a highly figurative conversation between Abraham and the rich man.

The figurative nature of this parable is self-evident by the fact that Abraham's chest cavity would be too small to fit heaven or a man into it, nor would crumbs and a water droplet provide much relief to a man in a furnace.

This story teaches that we only have one life to live, and our eternal destiny is determined by the choices we make during this life. Once we die, once we cross the gulf, there is no turning back. It also teaches that those who live a life of self-serving without God will find themselves like the rich man as outcasts from heaven. We are stewards on the earth and all our possessions belong to God and we will be held accountable for the use of these resources.

The rich man, as is typical of self, appears to blame God for his misfortune. When asking that one be resurrected from the dead to go and warn his family he was essentially saying "had you warned me adequately I would not be here." The answer was given that the information provided by the "law and the prophets" was adequate and that if they did not believe this, they would not believe one who rose from the dead. Lastly the rich man prayed to Abraham, but his petition was denied for Christ alone is a "Prince and a Saviour, for to give repentance to Israel, and forgiveness of sins." Acts 5:31. "Neither is there salvation in any other." Acts 4:12.

" **[10] The same shall drink of the wine of the wrath of God, which is poured out without mixture into the cup of his indignation; and he shall be tormented with fire and brimstone in the presence of the holy angels, and in the presence of the Lamb: [11] And the smoke of their torment ascendeth up for ever and ever: and they have no rest day nor night, who worship the beast and his**

**image, and whosoever receiveth the mark of his name."
Revelation 14:10, 11.**

The terms "forever" or "eternal" indicate a state of completion: "[7] Even as Sodom and Gomorrha, …suffering the vengeance of eternal fire." Jude 1:7. The fires of Sodom and Gomorrah have long been extinguished; once all that could be burned was burned the fire went out. The human frame is made of mostly carbon and once all has been consumed by fire, the fire goes out.

In ancient times brimstone or sulfur was the hottest burning substance known to man and was used to communicate the notion of intense energy. The fire or energy that destroys the wicked is likely of such intense heat - like an atomic explosion – that they are vaporized instantly. This is not a slow fire that gradually roasts the meat off their bones, this would be torture and is contrary to the nature of a loving Creator. "[11] …As I live, saith the Lord GOD, I have no pleasure in the death of the wicked;…" Ezekiel 33:11.

"And Jesus said unto him, Verily I say unto thee, To day shalt thou be with me in paradise." Luke 23:43

The verse appears to indicate by its punctuation that both Christ and the thief would be in paradise. Neither Christ nor the thief were in paradise that day as evident by the words of Christ on the morning of the resurrection. "[17] Jesus saith unto her, Touch me not; for I am not yet ascended to my Father:…"John 20:17

However, moving the second comma over one place the scripture would read "And Jesus said unto him, Verily I say

32

unto thee Today, shalt thou be with me in paradise."

In this verse Christ was inspiring faith in the penitent thief by underscoring the day of his own crucifixion as being at odds with his promise to give eternal life. "Today," the very day He was lifted between heaven and earth as a criminal, the very day His own disciples had forsaken Him, the very day the Jewish nation had rejected Him as King, on this very day, "today," against all apparent odds Christ assures the penitent thief of eternal life.

The Destruction of the Wicked

The sequence of events leading up to the destruction of the wicked is as follows: The first death comes to all of mankind **(the first death - Hebrews 9:27)**. When Christ returns those who are selfless will be resurrected to eternal life **(the first resurrection - 1 Thessalonians 4:16, 17.)** and will be taken to heaven where they will work with Christ for 1000 years **(Revelation 20: 5, 6)** and participate in the sentencing of the wicked. **(Revelation 20:4, 1 Corinthians 6:2)**

After the 1000 years of desolation on the earth the wicked will be resurrected **(second resurrection - Revelation 20:5),** they will be sentenced to death by fire that will consume them in an instant **(the second death - Revelation 21:18).** The earth is then purified with fire **(Malachi 4: 1-3),** thereafter the New Jerusalem will descend out of heaven uniting the family of earth with the family in heaven. **(Revelation 21: 1-7.)**

CHAPTER 5

MAN'S PRESCRIBED DIET

"[29] And God said, Behold, I have given you every herb bearing seed, which is upon the face of all the earth, and every tree, in the which is the fruit of a tree yielding seed; to you it shall be for meat. [30] And to every beast of the earth, and to every fowl of the air, and to every thing that creepeth upon the earth, wherein there is life, I have given every green herb for meat: and it was so." Genesis 1:29, 30.

In a world without death God provided a plant-based diet for both man and beast. On the 6th day of creation, the Divine Record indicates that grains ("herb bearing seed,") fruits and nuts ("tree yielding seed") were to be the menu.

"[17] And unto Adam he said, Because thou hast hearkened unto the voice of thy wife…cursed is the ground for thy sake; in sorrow shalt thou eat of it all the days of thy life; [18] Thorns also and thistles shall it bring forth to thee; and thou shalt eat the herb of the field;" Genesis 3:17, 18.

After the fall the plant-based diet was continued, however vegetables ("herb of the field") were now added to provide man with additional sustenance in the face of a sentence to hard labor.

"[1] And God blessed Noah and his sons, and said unto them, Be fruitful, and multiply, and replenish the earth. [2] And the fear of you and the dread of you shall be upon every beast of the earth, and upon every fowl of the air, upon all that moveth upon the earth, and upon all the fishes of the sea; into your hand are they delivered. [3]

Every moving thing that liveth shall be meat for you; even as the green herb have I given you all things.⁴ But flesh with the life thereof, which is the blood thereof, shall ye not eat." Genesis 9:1-4.

The most dramatic shift in man's diet came after the flood with the addition of flesh to sustain man in a world where all plant-based foods had been destroyed.

"⁴ But flesh with the life thereof, which is the blood thereof, shall ye not eat." Genesis 9:7.

The flesh that was permitted for consumption came with some exclusionary provisions. The consumed flesh must be drained of its blood since blood carries impurities. Today Jews call meat from a clean animal that has been drained of its blood as being "kosher." Cutting the animal's throat on a gradient and then allowing the animal's heart to pump out all the blood provides kosher meat. The apostle drew the attention to this method of meat preparation because the new pagan converts were accustomed to eating flesh with blood in it "²⁹ That ye abstain from meats offered to idols, and from blood, and from things strangled…" Acts 15:20.

"² Speak unto the children of Israel, saying, These are the beasts which ye shall eat among all the beasts that are on the earth.³ Whatsoever parteth the hoof, and is clovenfooted, and cheweth the cud, among the beasts, that shall ye eat.⁴ Nevertheless these shall ye not eat of them that chew the cud, or of them that divide the hoof: as the camel, because he cheweth the cud, but divideth not the hoof; he is unclean unto you…

"⁷ And the swine, though he divide the hoof, and be clovenfooted, yet he cheweth not the cud; he is unclean to you.⁸ Of their flesh shall ye not eat, and their carcase shall ye not touch; they are unclean to you." Leviticus 11: 2-4, 7,8**

The flesh-based diet following the flood was to come with further restrictions for health reasons; only animals labeled clean and fully drained of blood were permitted. The distinction between "clean" and "unclean" animals, or in modern day terms "healthy" and "unhealthy" is recorded in Leviticus 11 and Deuteronomy 14. These distinctions were certainly well known to Noah who was instructed to bring more clean animals than unclean animals into the ark (Genesis 7:2).

The Lord purposed that only grass eating animals (cud chewers) were permitted provided they had a cloven (divided) hoof such as sheep, cattle and deer but not those grass eaters that have a single hoof such as the horse. While pigs have a cloven hoof, they do not chew the cud and are hence rendered unclean or "unhealthy." The quality of pork meat is comparatively inferior due to their diet as they will eat virtually anything including decaying flesh.

"⁹ These shall ye eat of all that are in the waters: whatsoever hath fins and scales in the waters, in the seas, and in the rivers, them shall ye eat.¹⁰ And all that have not fins and scales in the seas, and in the rivers, of all that move in the waters, and of any living thing which is in the waters, they shall be an abomination unto you:" Leviticus 11:9,10

Similar distinctions were given for aquatic animals.

Aquatic animals that have scales and fins were deemed clean or "healthy" and thus permitted for consumption. Shrimp and crabs have neither; they are bottom feeders and like pigs consume all the waste at the bottom of the ocean rendering them unclean or "unhealthy." Insects, reptiles and birds of prey were also deemed unhealthy for consumption.

"^{23} And this I do for the gospel's sake, that I might be partaker thereof with you.^{24} Know ye not that they which run in a race run all, but one receiveth the prize? So run, that ye may obtain.^{25} And every man that striveth for the mastery is temperate in all things. Now they do it to obtain a corruptible crown; but we an incorruptible.^{26} I therefore so run, not as uncertainly; so fight I, not as one that beateth the air:" 1 Corinthians 9:23-26.

In the Book of Corinthians Paul compares a Christian's pursuit of a selfless character to an Olympic athlete training to win a gold medal, both in effort and technique. All who entered the games underwent exercise, good nutrition, adequate water intake and sufficient sleep. They were to be temperate, that is abstain from unhealthy foods and practices. Paul calls on God's people to be as persistent and to take care of their bodies as do these athletes, for athletes do it to obtain a perishable prize how much more should we whose reward is eternal life. "^{16} Know ye not that ye are the temple of God, and that the Spirit of God dwelleth in you? If any man defile the temple of God, him shall God destroy; for the temple of God is holy, which temple ye are." 1 Corinthians 3:16,17.

"^{6} The wolf also shall dwell with the lamb, and the leopard shall lie down with the kid; and the calf and the

young lion and the fatling together; and a little child shall lead them.[7] And the cow and the bear shall feed; their young ones shall lie down together: and the lion shall eat straw like the ox.[8] And the sucking child shall play on the hole of the asp, and the weaned child shall put his hand on the cockatrice' den.[9] They shall not hurt nor destroy in all my holy mountain: for the earth shall be full of the knowledge of the LORD, as the waters cover the sea." Isaiah 11: 6-9.

On the New Earth, God's original plan for man and beast will again be realized with a selfless plant-based diet.

SECTION II
THE FALL OF MAN

CHAPTER 6

THE EDEN HOME

The Tree of Knowledge of Good and Evil

"8 And the LORD God planted a garden eastward in Eden; and there he put the man whom he had formed. 9 And out of the ground made the LORD God to grow every tree that is pleasant to the sight, and good for food; the tree of life also in the midst of the garden, and the tree of knowledge of good and evil.

16 And the LORD God commanded the man, saying, Of every tree of the garden thou mayest freely eat: 17 But of the tree of the knowledge of good and evil, thou shalt not eat of it: for in the day that thou eatest thereof thou shalt surely die." Genesis 2: 8, 9, 16, 17

Amongst all the trees for food there were two distinct trees in the middle of the garden that came with specific instruction: the "tree of life" and the "tree of knowledge of good and evil." While they ate of the tree of life and abstained from the tree of knowledge, their immortality was maintained.

The "tree of knowledge of good and evil" was a literal tree bearing one kind of fruit. It gave man a choice between the two systems of government: Good (selflessness) vs. Evil (self-serving). Our first parents had been created under the government of God, a selfless government, and the only knowledge they knew was selfless cooperation with one another. They would remain under the Divine Administration so long as they refrained from the tree of knowledge and continued to eat from the tree of life.

However, were they to eat from the tree of knowledge they would fall under the government of Satan, a government of self-serving and its inevitable consequences of death.

The relationship between selflessness (good) leading to life vs. self-serving (evil) leading to death is not an arbitrary relationship ("do so because I said so") but rather a causal relationship (cause and effect). As a physician counsels against tobacco related lung cancer and death so God here warns our first parents against the dangers of self-serving and its consequential effect of death.

At creation all nature demonstrated this principle of selflessness, each creature working together for the good of all. In complex systems such as the human body this principle of selflessness is still largely present. Each organ of the human body works selflessly ensuring the survival of the entire organism. The lungs oxygenate the blood, the intestines fill the blood with nutrients, the liver filters the blood, and the heart pumps the blood around the body. If any of these systems selfishly hoarded the products of their labor the system would perish. It is in selfless cooperation, putting the interest of others first and foremost, that there is life.

The Creation of Eve & Her Marriage

"[18] And the LORD God said, It is not good that the man should be alone; I will make him an help meet for him. [19] And out of the ground the LORD God formed every beast of the field, and every fowl of the air; and brought them unto Adam to see what he would call them: and whatsoever Adam called every living creature, that was the name thereof. [20] And Adam gave names to all cattle, and to the fowl of the air, and to every beast of the field;

41

but for Adam there was not found an help meet for him.

²¹ And the LORD God caused a deep sleep to fall upon Adam, and he slept: and he took one of his ribs, and closed up the flesh instead thereof; ²² And the rib, which the LORD God had taken from man, made he a woman, and brought her unto the man. ²³ And Adam said, This is now bone of my bones, and flesh of my flesh: she shall be called Woman, because she was taken out of Man.²⁴ Therefore shall a man leave his father and his mother, and shall cleave unto his wife: and they shall be one flesh.²⁵ And they were both naked, the man and his wife, and were not ashamed." Genesis 2: 18-25.

Despite the companionship of the animals and communion with God, Adam was lonely without an equal. Adam's rib was to be the basic material from which Eve was to be created. The words "…and brought her unto the man" indicate that God celebrated the first marriage. The covenant of marriage is a covenant of God that exists between a man and a woman.

At the marriage ceremony God now pronounces man to leave his father and his mother to unite physically and spiritually with his wife holding up monogamy before the world as the form of marriage ordained by God. These words do not recommend a forsaking of one's duty toward parents, but man would take on a new relationship, his primary affections and duty would be toward his wife. Adam and Eve, husband and wife were to become "one flesh." These words express unity of body and interests. The Savior uses this very passage in His strongest condemnation of divorce. "⁵ And said, For this cause shall a man leave father and mother, and shall cleave to his wife: and they twain shall be one flesh? ⁶ Wherefore they are no more twain, but one flesh. What therefore God hath joined together, let not man put asunder." Mathew 19: 5,6.

Divorce was never in God's plan but was permitted only for infidelity, the indulgence of selfishness. "[7] They say unto him, Why did Moses then command to give a writing of divorcement, and to put her away? [8] He saith unto them, Moses because of the hardness of your hearts suffered you to put away your wives: but from the beginning it was not so. [9] And I say unto you, Whosoever shall put away his wife, except it be for fornication, and shall marry another, committeth adultery: and whoso marrieth her which is put away doth commit adultery." Mathew 19: 7-9.

The relationship between husband and wife is compared to the relationship that Christ has with the church, the nuclear family unit. Christ directs the family unit through the father. As the father of the family unit is subject to Christ so the wife is subject to the husband. As Christ cares for the family unit so the husband is to care for the wife.

"[22] Wives, submit yourselves unto your own husbands, as unto the Lord.[23] For the husband is the head of the wife, even as Christ is the head of the church: and he is the saviour of the body.[24] Therefore as the church is subject unto Christ, so let the wives be to their own husbands in every thing. "[25] Husbands, love your wives, even as Christ also loved the church, and gave himself for it;… [28] So ought men to love their wives as their own bodies. He that loveth his wife loveth himself.[29] For no man ever yet hated his own flesh; but nourisheth and cherisheth it, even as the Lord the church:" Ephesians 5:22-25, 28, 29.

Men are to love their wives in selflessness putting the best interests of their spouse in front of their own. A marriage relationship where selflessness reigns supreme is a harmonious relationship. It is appropriate that the scriptures first bring to view the tree of knowledge before the discussion of the marriage relationship thus pointing out the secret of a harmonious marriage - abstinence from the tree of self-serving. Discord is rooted in a clash of wills which is rooted in SELF.

CHAPTER 7
THE FALL OF MAN

"¹ Now the serpent was more subtil than any beast of the field which the LORD God had made. And he said unto the woman, Yea, hath God said, Ye shall not eat of every tree of the garden?" Genesis 3:1.

God had cautioned our first parents: "thou shalt not" eat of the tree of knowledge of good and evil for the result would be: "thou shalt surely die" Genesis 2:17. Satan now restates God's clear command "thou shalt not," as an ambiguous question bringing doubt to Eve's mind: "Did God really say: 'You must not eat from any tree in the garden?'" OR "Are there any trees in the garden of which you may not eat?" The Hebrew words spoken by the serpent are ambiguous and therefore allow for both translations.

Satan was trying to confuse Eve. His words were intended to be ambiguous for the purpose of placing doubt in her mind concerning the exact phrase and the exact meaning of what God had said leading her to question whether the instruction was reasonable.

Eve was now presented with a problem and her subconscious mind began to reason. "Why can we eat from all the millions of trees except one? That makes no sense, there must be a reason for this…. and of all the trees it's the one right in the middle…I wonder if it's forbidden because of its location and why does this tree alone cause death..." With one ambiguous question Satan raised numerous questions in Eve's mind for which she was now seeking an answer. This simple question of Satan is a masterpiece of deception and in this the serpent was more cunning than any "beast of the field." It is only the forked tongue of the serpent that speaks in ambiguity, "…let your yea be yea; and your nay, nay; …" James 5:12.

"**² And the woman said unto the serpent, We may eat of the fruit of the trees of the garden: ³ But of the fruit of the tree which is in the midst of the garden, God hath said, Ye shall not eat of it, neither shall ye touch it, <u>lest</u> ye die." Genesis 3:2, 3.**

Eve evidently understood the question in the second sense and changed what God had said from a certainty "thou shalt surely die" to a possibility, "lest ye die" indicating some contingency or extenuating circumstance that may avert certain death. While knowing the name of the tree she simply refers to it as the tree in the "midst" of the garden thus placing it in the same class with the other trees in the garden. Thus, the words of God were neutralized.

"**⁴ And the serpent said unto the woman, Ye shall not surely die: ⁵ For God doth know that in the day ye eat thereof, then your eyes shall be opened, and ye shall be as gods, knowing good and evil." Genesis 3:4, 5.**

Satan's first question, which was delivered to arouse doubt, is now followed up with a deceptive authoritative statement: "You will positively not die," thus challenging the truthfulness of God's Word in an open lie. Eve was questioning in her mind how this could be that they could eat of all the trees except one, illogical and unexplained. Satan now supplies a reasonable explanation for the prohibition; "You can be sure, you can count on it, it's not through any fear of you dying but through fear of you becoming competitors to your Maker."

Satan insinuated that the death sentence "given" by God was arbitrary for the purpose of maintaining His position as Ruler of the Universe. By eating this fruit, she would in fact become like God. No longer would she have God's Fatherly providence to guide her, she would oversee herself, her own destiny, doing and acting as she pleased. By eating the fruit, she would achieve her full potential and reach godhood. She would no longer be a slave to God's system of "oppressive" government.

"⁶ And when the woman saw that the tree was good for food, and that it was pleasant to the eyes, and a tree to be desired to make one wise, she took of the fruit thereof, and did eat, and gave also unto her husband with her; and he did eat. Genesis 3:6.

After doubt in God's selfless motives took hold, the tree now seemed more inviting, it appealed to her taste, her vision and a desire for wisdom. Eve was already guilty in her mind of breaking the divine command "thou shalt not covet." Next, she violated the 8th commandment "thou shalt not steal." By giving it to her husband she violated the 6th commandment "thou shalt not kill." She also broke the 1st commandment because she placed Satan before God. The underlying principle of the 10 Commandments is selflessness, it is self-serving that leads to harm and it's against this harm the commandants give warning.

Eve had been created, as a "help meet" for her husband, but she now becomes the cause of his destruction. "Adam was not deceived, but the women" 1 Timothy 2:14. His love for her led him to eat the fruit. The thought of her dying was too much for him to bear and instead of waiting to discuss the matter with God he took his fate into his own hands and did eat.

Adams fall was a greater tragedy for he was not deceived, and he did not doubt God's selfless character, but he acted impulsively. It was the deliberate choice of Adam that made death the inevitable lot of mankind. We may speculate had Adam remained faithful, Christ would have died for Eve, once justified she would have been restored to Adam before they brought children into the world, thus averting our current state of sinful existence.

"⁷ And the eyes of them both were opened, and they knew that they were naked; and they sewed fig leaves together, and made themselves aprons.⁸ And they heard the voice of the LORD God walking in the garden in the cool of the day: and Adam and his wife hid themselves from the presence of the LORD God amongst the trees of the garden.⁹ And the LORD God called unto Adam, and said unto him, Where art thou?¹⁰ And he said, I heard thy voice in the garden, and I was afraid, because I was naked; and I hid myself." Genesis 3:7-10

Their "eyes were opened" they became "SELF-AWARE" the principle of SELF was now awakened and they saw themselves as being naked. Indeed, how sad was this eye opening, in love God had given them a knowledge of selflessness and its inevitable results of life and happiness (good) but now they were to experience the inevitable results of self-serving (evil); pain, suffering and death.

"¹¹ And he said, Who told thee that thou wast naked? Hast thou eaten of the tree, whereof I commanded thee that thou shouldest not eat?¹² And the man said, The woman whom thou gavest to be with me, she gave me of

the tree, and I did eat.[13] And the L ORD God said unto the woman, What is this that thou hast done? And the woman said, The serpent beguiled me, and I did eat." Genesis 3:11-13.

The moment they had eaten the fruit their natures were changed from selfless to self-serving. Adam with the new tendency of self-preservation now blames the woman, "that thou gavest," hence indirectly God Himself. The woman too in the mode of self-preservation in turn blames the serpent, which God had evidently permitted into the garden. Each excuse was designed for self-preservation. Our first parents now became agents of Satan in casting blame on God for their actions. This is in sharp contrast to Christ who selflessly carried our sin and penalty, even to death, for in Him is no selfishness.

CHAPTER 8

THE PLAN OF REDEMPTION

The Promise of a Deliverer.

"I will put enmity between thee and the woman, and between thy seed and her seed; it shall bruise thy head, and thou shalt bruise His heel." Genesis 3:15.

Turning to the serpent, the Lord now pronounces judgment on the Devil: Paraphrasing: "I will put enmity between thee **(you the devil)** and the woman **(Eve),** and between thy seed **(the followers of Satan)** and her seed **(Eve's descendants)**; it **(the Messiah, the pre-eminent "seed" Galatians 3:16)** shall bruise thy head, and thou shalt bruise His heel." Genesis 3:15.

Downcast from their fall, God lovingly gives them a promise of hope. The "enmity" spoken of here is a natural antagonism that exists between those who are selfless and those who are servants of self. The nail prints in the hands and feet of Christ, the scar in His side will be eternal reminders of the battle in which the serpent bruised the heel of the woman's seed. (John 20:25). The plan however to rescue man was not an afterthought but was conceived before the creation of the world to meet an emergency should it exist; it was "[25] …the revelation of the mystery, which was kept secret since the world began." Romans 16:25.

Christ was not only to redeem man but also the earth. The earth and its wildlife had been entrusted to Adam, but through his sin he had forfeited his home to the enemy who claimed to be "the god of this world." 2 Corinthians 4:4.

Christ's sacrifice would not only cancel Adams's debt and restore his human nature to selflessness, but He would also recover his lost home. Paul described this restoration as "the redemption of the purchased possession." Ephesians 1:14.

God's creatures that share the "breath of life" in common with man are innocent of the fall but suffer because of man's choice and will benefit equally from man's restoration. God in His might calls the stars by name (Psalms 147:4), He numbers the dust of the earth (Isaiah 40:12) and is mindful when His precious sparrows sing their last (Mathew 10:29). These creatures that have suffered neglect and cruelty at the hand of man will be restored and will have a voice with our Father on that Day of Final Accounts!

God Parents His Children

"[16] Unto the woman he said, I will greatly multiply thy sorrow and thy conception; in sorrow thou shalt bring forth children; and thy desire shall be to thy husband, and he shall rule over thee.[17] And unto Adam he said, Because thou hast hearkened unto the voice of thy wife, and hast eaten of the tree, of which I commanded thee, saying, Thou shalt not eat of it: cursed is the ground for thy sake; in sorrow shalt thou eat of it all the days of thy life;[18] Thorns also and thistles shall it bring forth to thee; and thou shalt eat the herb of the field; [19] In the sweat of thy face shalt thou eat bread, till thou return unto the ground; for out of it wast thou taken: for dust thou art, and unto dust shalt thou return." Genesis 3:16-19

God was not to abandon his children, but in selfless love He would set in motion a plan that would bring them back to Himself by canceling their debt and restoring in them a

51

selfless character. Now that their nature had been infected with self-serving, they were to be expelled from Eden as the relative ease of the garden would only foster this self-serving trait. A life of discipline and hard work would aid in keeping this selfish tendency in check. The self-serving heart desires nothing more than a life of ease: "[49] Behold, this was the iniquity of thy sister Sodom, pride, fullness of bread, and abundance of idleness ..." Ezekiel 16:49.

For women in their domain of operation there were to be challenges. Motherhood is a tireless and selfless work; from morning to night there is no reprieve. There is no glory in doing the cooking, cleaning, washing, diaper changes and child education. A woman's desire would be for her husband as a balancing force. Many women today who work in the world suffer depression apart from their husbands.

For men their work in the field would not be easy. There would be thorns and thistles to keep a life of ease in check. Today one unexpected bill after another is like thorns and thistles that creep up unexpectedly. Human nature is always ready to complain as the desire for ease is placed in check.

The Devil had chosen a path of self-serving having a full knowledge of the selfless character of God. There was nothing God could do to save him, but our first parents were deceived and as such God would set in motion His plan to save them. Adam and Eve would now leave their home and embark on a journey. Though hard, it would ultimately lead them back to the arms of a loving Father who would spare nothing for their salvation, even sacrificing Himself in the person of His Son.

"²⁰ And Adam called his wife's name Eve; because she was the mother of all living.²¹ Unto Adam also and to his wife did the LORD God make coats of skins, and clothed them.²² And the LORD God said, Behold, the man is become as one of us, to know good and evil: and now, lest he put forth his hand, and take also of the tree of life, and eat, and live for ever: ²³ Therefore the LORD God sent him forth from the garden of Eden, to till the ground from whence he was taken.²⁴ So he drove out the man; and he placed at the east of the garden of Eden Cherubims, and a flaming sword which turned every way, to keep the way of the tree of life." Genesis 3:20-24

To prevent mankind from becoming a race of immortal sinners God placed angels at the entrance to the garden to prevent their access to the tree of life. The garden was presumably transplanted to heaven at some point prior to the flood to be restored to Adam and his family at a future date: "And he shewed me a pure river of water of life, clear as crystal, proceeding out of the throne of God and of the Lamb. ² In the midst of the street of it, and on either side of the river, was there the tree of life, which bare twelve manner of fruits, and yielded her fruit every month: and the leaves of the tree were for the healing of the nations." Revelation 22: 1, 2.

The 4 basic rules of parenting as per God's example demonstrated in Eden:

1) Clear communication of rules and expectations – do not eat of the tree.

2) Clear communication of the consequences – eating leads to death.

3) Keeping consistent accountability – expulsion from the garden.

4) Discipline in selflessness (love & patience) - promise of a redeemer.

God's actions in dealing with our first parents is a blueprint for parents today as they correct their children in sanctification. Any child who is not held accountable for their actions will only grow head strong in the spirit of self-serving. Had God not held them accountable, had He felt "sorry" for them (as parents often do today), he would have permitted them to stay in the garden and the result would have been immortal sinners with subsequent chaos throughout the universe. Parents who do not hold their children accountable suffer chaos in their homes and their children struggle as adults to attain a selfless character.

"Those who spare the rod of discipline hate their children. Those who love their children care enough to discipline them." Proverbs 13:24 (New Living Translation). The rod spoken of here is not the lash but a mere symbol of discipline which can take on the form of a restriction of privileges. God restricted Adam and Eve's privilege to the tree of life, he did not beat them. This Bible verse does not sanction corporal punishment, as aggression only fosters aggression. As God expelled them from the garden in love, He gave them hope of return through the promise of His Son. All true parental correction will reflect the spirit of selflessness.

CHAPTER 9
THE NATURE OF REBELLION
The Rebellion in Heaven

"[12] How art thou fallen from heaven, O Lucifer, son of the morning! how art thou cut down to the ground, which didst weaken the nations![13] For thou hast said in thine heart, I will ascend into heaven, I will exalt my throne above the stars of God: I will sit also upon the mount of the congregation, in the sides of the north:[14] I will ascend above the heights of the clouds; I will be like the most High." Isaiah 14:12-14.

From eternity God has governed the universe by the great Law of Selflessness of which the Ten Commandments are an abbreviated form. While this principle of placing others first and foremost was practiced there was peace and harmony throughout the universe. Lucifer however, an angel of immense intelligence and beauty, broke this law by conspiring to unseat God from the throne of the universe and establish an administration built on the principle of self-service.

Vanity and a thirst for power drove Lucifer to covet his Makers position " [12] … Thou sealest up the sum, full of wisdom, and perfect in beauty.[13] Thou hast been in Eden the garden of God; every precious stone was thy covering,…..[14] Thou art the anointed cherub that covereth; and I have set thee so: thou wast upon the holy mountain of God; thou hast walked up and down in the midst of the stones of fire. [15] Thou wast perfect in thy ways from the day that thou wast created, till iniquity was found in thee.[16] …and thou hast sinned: therefore I will cast thee as profane out of the mountain of God: and I will destroy thee, O covering cherub, from the midst of the stones of fire.[17] Thine heart was lifted up because of thy beauty, thou hast corrupted thy wisdom by reason of thy brightness: …Ezekiel 28:12-17.

Eve had been deceived, but Lucifer and his angels had full knowledge of God's selfless character and as such there was nothing God could do to save them. God could have destroyed Lucifer and his followers but without giving him time to demonstrate the workings of his government their destruction would lead to an unacceptable form of fear-motivated service. Time was to be given to Lucifer to establish his self-serving government so that all might make an informed decision on whom they would serve.

But to maintain stability of the existing government the insurgents were expelled from heaven. "[7] And there was war in heaven: Michael and his angels fought against the dragon; and the dragon fought and his angels, [8] And prevailed not; neither was their place found any more in heaven.[9] And the great dragon was cast out, that old serpent, called the Devil, and Satan, which deceiveth the whole world: he was cast out into the earth, and his angels were cast out with him." Revelation 12: 7-9. Michael who is none other than Christ Himself (Jude 1:9, Daniel 12:1) led out the battle in expelling the insurgents from heaven.

After Satan came to the earth with his rebel angels, he implemented the next phase of his plan; obtain a following amongst the human race. Satan well knew of God's selfless love for His creatures, and he certainly counted on Christ risking his life to save them. If he could thus force Christ from the throne to save man and overcome Him, then the throne would be vacated and his for the taking. Satan was not deceived but calculated. Accordingly, his name Lucifer, which means light bearer, was changed to Satan, which means deceiver.

The Climax of the Rebellion

"**[30]** **When Jesus therefore had received the vinegar, he said, It is finished: and he bowed his head, and gave up the ghost.:...**" John 19:30.

From the very beginning the inhabitants of heaven had witnessed Satan's rebellion, but in the life and death of Christ, Satan's true motives were revealed. All of heaven watched the Savior as He was arrested at midnight and rushed through the streets of Jerusalem. They saw Him charged twice before the priests, twice before Pilate and once before Herod. They saw Him, the King of heaven, arraigned by Herod in an old scarlet robe (Luke 23:11), they beheld their Lord wearing a crown of thorns (John 19:2) before being crucified.

Everything to try the soul of a man to indulge in self-preservation was invented by Satan and his angels. But all the beatings, mockery, betrayal, abandonment, and the horrors of a crucifixion could not force that Selfless Soul into self-preservation. Alone and abandoned of God, Christ died bearing the full penalty of man's transgressions. In Christ's death upon Calvary, it was shown that Satan's true motive was not to liberate man from a supposed dictatorship but to murder the Son of God and then seize the throne.

Before the sacrifice of Christ neither men nor angels were safe from rebellion. The Cross of Christ will forever be the antidote against the spirit of self-serving for if any should think to revive the Devil's claims the cross will be the reminder as to the terrible consequences of self-serving and the infinite price paid for our redemption.

For the past six thousand years this rebellion has raged on in the hearts and minds of men, but when the contest shall be over the character of God will be vindicated before men and angels. It will finally be clear that the Law of Selflessness is the source of security for the entire universe. The extermination of the self-serving one and his ideology will demonstrate that God has acted with the best interests of the universe at heart. So poignant were those dying yet triumphant words of Christ the King when he cried out; "It is finished."

The Law of God

"[31] Behold, the days come, saith the LORD, that I will make a new covenant with the house of Israel, ... I will put my law in their inward parts, and write it in their hearts; and will be their God, and they shall be my people.[34] And they shall teach no more every man his neighbour, and every man his brother, saying, Know the LORD: for they shall all know me, from the least of them unto the greatest of them, ..." Jeremiah 31:31-34.

The Law of God, selflessness, was written in the hearts and minds of His creatures at the time they were created. Following the fall of our first parents this instinct of selflessness was gradually replaced by the instinct of self-serving. Through the centuries as selflessness faded from the heart it became necessary for God to write down on stone an abbreviated form of this great principle in the form of the 10 Commandments, which men would then read and apply to their hearts within.

The law written in stone and given to Israel formed the basis of the "Old Covenant." The Israelites pledged obedience to the law and in turn God would be their God and they would be His special people. (Exodus19:5, Exodus 24:7). The written law was much like a tutor where men could read the law and apply it to the heart within. When Christ came and established the "New Covenant" the law was no longer to be written in stone, but in the heart by the Holy Spirit, as it had been in Eden.

The Law of Selflessness is exhaustless; yelling at one's spouse or children is not defined by the 10 Commandments, but it is covered under the great Law of Selflessness for yelling is of self; therefore, yelling is a transgression of The Law. The Law of Selflessness and hence its abbreviated form of 10 Commandments was given for the purpose of harm reduction: defrauding one's neighbor, taking another man's wife all cause harm. Selflessness is placing the best interest of others first and foremost.

Paul in the New Testament refers to the great "Law of Selflessness" as the "spirit of the law" and its abbreviated form of the 10 Commandments as the "letter of the law" (Romans 7:6, 2 Corinthians 3:6). Christ explained that killing a man is a transgression of the letter of the law, but hating a man in one's heart is a violation of the "the spirit of the law," that great Law of Selflessness" (Mathew 5:21-28).

The condition of eternal life today is the same as it was in Eden, complete reflection of the great Law of Selflessness. In today's modern-day language "obedience" means "compliance" and implies an active process as under the Old Covenant. Rather we are to be "reflectors" of that Law which implies a passive process since this reflection is the work of the Holy Spirit as under the New Covenant. Under the Old Covenant Israel was to be "obedient" to the Law of Selflessness. Under the New Covenant as spiritual Jews we are to be "reflectors" of the Law of Selflessness.

The ark containing the Ten Commandments, the great embodiment of the Law of Selflessness, is seen by John in the temple in heaven (Revelation 11:19). The ark is to remain as a testament throughout eternity as to the selfless nature of God's government, for "sin is the transgression of the law" 1 John 3:4 and "wages of sin is death." Romans 6:23. Since the Law is Selflessness, any form of self-serving is therefore sin.

SECTION III
THE CORRUPTION
OF THE EARTH

CHAPTER 10
THE TWO SEEDS, CAIN AND ABEL

The Seed of the Serpent

"¹ And Adam knew Eve his wife; and she conceived, and bare Cain, and said, I have gotten a man from the LORD. ² And she again bare his brother Abel. And Abel was a keeper of sheep, but Cain was a tiller of the ground.

³ And in process of time it came to pass, that Cain brought of the fruit of the ground an offering unto the LORD.⁴ And Abel, he also brought of the firstlings of his flock and of the fat thereof. And the LORD had respect unto Abel and to his offering: ⁵ But unto Cain and to his offering he had not respect. And Cain was very wroth, and his countenance fell." Genesis 4:1-5.

In the process of time the two sons of Adam brought their sin offerings before the Lord. The younger, Abel brought a firstling from his flock together with its fat as prescribed by the law of sacrifices (Leviticus 4:1-8). Cain brought an offering of fruit. Abel's sacrificial offering, which pointed toward the great sacrifice of Christ, was accepted but Cain's bloodless offering of fruit was rejected.

The sacrificial system was instituted so that man could be forgiven his sin by means of a substitute. Christ alone could be this substitute for He is the source and essence of the Law of Selflessness with life that is eternal. Animal sacrifices were instituted temporarily as an "I owe you" until Christ should come and pay that debt with His life. There was no merit in the blood of an animal to forgive sin;

it was only symbolic of the sacrifice of Christ. All sins were forgiven based upon the future sacrifice of Christ.

"⁶ And the LORD said unto Cain, Why art thou wroth? and why is thy countenance fallen?⁷ If thou doest well, shalt thou not be accepted? and if thou doest not well, sin lieth at the door. And unto thee shall be his desire, and thou shalt rule over him." Genesis 4:6, 7

God as a loving parent now reasons with Cain showing him that if he followed the divine direction regarding the law of sacrifices then there would be no need for correction and Cain would no longer have a reason to show a disappointed and angry face. God warns Cain that if he failed to reign in and bridle himself, self like a wild beast would overtake him. Physical or verbal aggression is an expression of self and is here personified as a wild beast lying in wait. "And unto thee shall be his desire" or as the Revised Standard Version translates: "its desire is for you, but you must master it."

"⁸ And Cain talked with Abel his brother: and it came to pass, when they were in the field, that Cain rose up against Abel his brother, and slew him." Genesis 4:8.

Out in the field the two brothers argued, the content of their conversion is unknown, but Cain likely accused God of being unfair with him and Abel coming in defense of God. The natural antagonism ("enmity") that would exist between good (selflessness) and evil (self-serving) as described in Eden (Genesis 3:15) was realized when Cain killed his brother.

Here we see the contrast of the two distinct seeds within humanity: those who are selfless are willing to follow the divine direction no matter the request or cost, deferring all to God's divine foresight and perfect judgment knowing and believing that God places our best interest first and foremost. Those who are self-serving believe in their own finite wisdom and charter their own course thus believing the words of the serpent "ye shall be as gods." Genesis 3:5. The New Testament refers to these two seeds as the "wheat and the tares" (Mathew 13:24-30).

"⁹ And the LORD said unto Cain, Where is Abel thy brother? And he said, I know not: Am I my brother's keeper? ¹⁰ And he said, What hast thou done? the voice of thy brother's blood crieth unto me from the ground." Genesis 4:9, 10.

God now gives Cain an opportunity to repent that he might create in him a new heart, but Cain denied his guilt and added falsehood to murder. The call to repentance having been rejected God now charges Cain with the crime of murder. Self becomes so self-centered that the omnipotence of God's presence is forgotten.

"¹¹ And now art thou cursed from the earth, which hath opened her mouth to receive thy brother's blood from thy hand; ¹² When thou tillest the ground, it shall not henceforth yield unto thee her strength; a fugitive and a vagabond shalt thou be in the earth." Genesis 4:11,12.

Following the fall of our first parents, God "cursed" the ground with "thorns and thistles," a loving measure to keep the selfish ease-loving nature in check. The earth's yielding capacity was again to be reduced in a further disciplinary measure to curb the growing selfish heart that had now

64

resorted to murder. Self is always restless and in search of something new and better and by his own choice Cain would wander from place to place in search of novelty much like men do today.

"13 And Cain said unto the LORD, My punishment is greater than I can bear. 14 Behold, thou hast driven me out this day from the face of the earth; and it shall come to pass, that every one that findeth me shall slay me." Genesis 4:13, 14

Cain had just murdered his brother, yet there was no word of sorrow, no recognition of guilt or shame. Instead of confessing he complains; "my punishment is greater than I can bear." Self always whines about how unfairly it has been treated and lacks any form of accountability and is always ready to point the finger. Adam had blamed God for giving him the woman, the woman had blamed God for permitting the serpent into the garden and now Cain blames God for driving him out. Cain drove himself out from the presence of God for selfishness cannot dwell with selflessness, they are two polarizing forces.

"15 And the LORD said unto him, Therefore whosoever slayeth Cain, vengeance shall be taken on him sevenfold. And the LORD set a mark upon Cain, lest any finding him should kill him. 16 And Cain went out from the presence of the LORD, and dwelt in the land of Nod, on the east of Eden." Genesis 4:15,16.

The mark placed upon Cain was not a visible mark but a seal of God's protection, if any should kill Cain, they would suffer the full consequence "seven-fold" as he himself was suffering for the killing of his brother. Though Cain was rejected, God was still to be the defender of the right and as such Cain was not to be abandoned to the enemy. "Vengeance is mine; I will repay, saith the Lord." Romans 12:19.

The Seed of the Women

"³ And Adam lived an hundred and thirty years, and begat a son in his own likeness, and after his image; and called his name Seth: ⁴ And the days of Adam after he had begotten Seth were eight hundred years: and he begat sons and daughters: ⁵ And all the days that Adam lived were nine hundred and thirty years: and he died." Genesis 5:3-5.**

Adam and Eve welcomed Seth, the first of a line of men after the death of Abel, through whom the Messiah the pre-eminent seed would come. Seth was not without character defects having inherited Adam's fallen self-serving nature, a trait he would need to master. Adam was 130 years old when Seth was born, and he lived another 800 years. Adam died when he was 930 years old.

"⁶ And Seth lived an hundred and five years, and begat Enos:…" Genesis 5:6.

Seth was 105 years old when he had his first son, Enos. Genesis Chapter 5 gives the chronology of Adam's offspring, the ages at which their sons were born, and their deaths as tabulated below. From the table we can calculate that Adam died 726 years before the flood.

Adam's Genealogy (Genesis 5)		
	Age at sons' birth	Age at death
Adam	130	930
Seth	105	912
Enos	90	905
Cainan	70	910
Mahalaleel	65	895
Jared	162	962
Enoch	65	365/translated
Methuselah	187	969
Lamech	182	777
Noah	500	950
	=1556 years	

By the addition of ages at which the firstborn sons were born we can calculate that it was 1556 years from creation to the birth of Noah's son, when Noah was 500 years old. Noah was, however, 600 years old when he entered the ark. Thus, an additional 100 years is to be added to calculate the time from creation to the actual flood, which would be 1656 years.

[22] And Enoch walked with God after he begat Methuselah three hundred years, and begat sons and daughters: [23] And all the days of Enoch were three hundred sixty and five years: [24] And Enoch walked with God: and he was not; for God took him." Genesis 5:22-24.

The most notable descendant between Adam and Noah was Enoch. "[14] And Enoch also, the seventh from Adam,

67

prophesied of these, saying, Behold, the Lord cometh with ten thousands of his saints, [15] To execute judgment upon all, and to convince all that are ungodly among them of all their ungodly deeds which they have ungodly committed, and of all their hard speeches which ungodly sinners have spoken against him." Jude 1:14,15.

Enoch warned the "ungodly," those who are "not like God," that is those who are "self-serving," of the second coming of Christ. Synonyms are: Godly – selfless – good – righteous vs. ungodly – self-serving – evil – unrighteous. Enoch's message was for men to turn from their self-serving lives and to reflect the selfless character of God that they might stand the test of judgment. Enoch was 365 years old when he was translated to heaven without seeing death.

CHAPTER 11

DISSOLUTION OF THE FAMILY UNIT

Intermixing of the Two Seeds

"[1]And it came to pass, when men began to multiply on the face of the earth, and daughters were born unto them, [2] That the sons of God saw the daughters of men that they were fair; and they took them wives of all which they chose." Genesis 6:1, 2.

The selfless descendants of Seth, "The sons of God," and the self-serving descendants of Cain, "the daughters of men," now began to intermarry taking themselves wives not for virtue but beauty.

"[3] And the LORD said, My spirit shall not always strive with man, for that he also is flesh: yet his days shall be an hundred and twenty years." Genesis 6:3

This union between the selfless Sethites and self-serving Cainites, the two seeds within humanity, soon lead to dissolution of the nuclear family unit with its inevitable results of a violent lawless society. God foresaw that it would be 120 years before men would reach the point of no return, a point where they had fully committed themselves in the service of self.

"[4] There were giants in the earth in those days; and also after that, when the sons of God came in unto the daughters of men, and they bare children to them, the same became mighty men which were of old, men of renown.[5] And God saw that the wickedness of man was great in the earth, and that every imagination of the

thoughts of his heart was only evil continually." Genesis 6:4-6.

The results of the unions between the Sethites and the Cainites were "giants," from the Hebrew word "Nephilim," which comes from the word "naphal" meaning "violent one." Violence is the complete expression of self.

God had designed for each family unit to be governed by selfless parents under the direction of a selfless God. However, when there are two parents each having their own set of values and rules (selflessness vs self-serving), children grow up to be oppositional, defiant, lacking respect and boundaries taking anything they desire when told "no," even by force. The end results in a lawless family and a lawless society.

The Nuclear Family Unit as the Church

The "church" is traditionally conceptualized as an organization between four walls to be attended to once a week. This model of centralized worship is based upon the old pagan form of temple worship. While its true God did institute a central form of worship in Jerusalem it was nevertheless temporary until Christ should come. The Temple in Jerusalem was designed to teach men the way of Holiness (selflessness) until the Holy Spirit should come. Thereafter every person was to become a temple of the Holy Spirit (1 Corinthians 6:19) and every family a church where the religion of the Bible can be practiced thus bringing man back to the original plan as it was in Eden.

Each family unit in turn was to become a member of God's invisible church by reflection of the Divine selfless character. The Great Church of God is invisible and eternal transcending the ages: "[5] Ye also, as lively stones, are built up a spiritual house, an holy priesthood, to offer up spiritual sacrifices, acceptable to God by Jesus Christ."1 Peter 2: 5.

Jesus referenced this transition away from centralized worship in His conversation with a woman of Samaria whom He met at Jacobs Well. She asked the question: "[20] Our fathers worshipped in this mountain; and ye say, that in Jerusalem is the place where men ought to worship.[21] Jesus saith unto her, Woman, believe me, the hour cometh, when ye shall neither in this mountain, nor yet at Jerusalem, worship the Father.[23] But the hour cometh, and now is, when the true worshippers shall worship the Father in spirit and in truth: for the Father seeketh such to worship him.[24] God is a Spirit: and they that worship him must worship him in spirit and in truth." John 4:20-24.

Under the New Covenant when the Holy Spirit writes the Law of Selflessness on the heart, there is no need for any external form of state or federal government to control behavior. Man made government becomes a necessity when the human heart is void of the Holy Spirit. The restoration of the church in the form of the nuclear family unit is the great object of the gospel. This restoration is foretold by Malachi: "[5] Behold, I will send you Elijah the prophet before the coming of the great and dreadful day of the LORD:[6] And he shall turn the heart of the fathers to the children, and the heart of the children to their fathers, lest I come and smite the earth with a curse." Malachi 4:5, 6.

The Family Unit as a School

The family was also to function as a school where children worked alongside their parents learning the skills of life. Nature was to be their classroom. Sadly, today children are sent to school in an artificial environment where they are educated and raised by strangers in the service of self; the result is often a selfish, demanding, oppositional, entitled, and aggressive child.

Protective Separation

The union of the selfless with the self-serving led to the dissolution of the nuclear family unit. The necessity of protective separation is documented in both Old and New Testaments:

"[2] ...thou shalt make no covenant with them, nor shew mercy unto them: [3] Neither shalt thou make marriages with them; thy daughter thou shalt not give unto his son, nor his daughter shalt thou take unto thy son.[4] For they will turn away thy son from following me,

that they may serve other gods: so will the anger of the LORD be kindled against you, and destroy thee suddenly.[5] But thus shall ye deal with them; ye shall destroy their altars, and break down their images, and cut down their groves, and burn their graven images with fire.[6] For thou art an holy people unto the LORD thy God: the LORD thy God hath chosen thee to be a special people unto himself, above all people that are upon the face of the earth." Deuteronomy 7:2-6.

"[14] Be ye not unequally yoked together with unbelievers: for what fellowship hath righteousness with unrighteousness? and what communion hath light with darkness?[15] And what concord hath Christ with Belial? or what part hath he that believeth with an infidel?[16] And what agreement hath the temple of God with idols? for ye are the temple of the living God; as God hath said, I will dwell in them, and walk in them; and I will be their God, and they shall be my people.[17] Wherefore come out from among them, and be ye separate, saith the Lord, and touch not the unclean thing; and I will receive you,[18] And will be a Father unto you, and ye shall be my sons and daughters, saith the Lord Almighty."2 Corinthian's 6: 14-18.

"[9] I wrote unto you in an epistle not to company with fornicators: [10] Yet not altogether with the fornicators of this world, or with the covetous, or extortioners, or with idolaters; for then must ye needs go out of the world.[11] But now I have written unto you not to keep company, if any man that is called a brother be a fornicator, or covetous, or an idolater, or a railer, or a drunkard, or an extortioner; with such an one no not to eat.[12] For what have I to do to judge them also that are without? do not ye judge them that are within?[13] But them that are without God judgeth. Therefore put away from among yourselves that wicked person." 1 Corinthians 5:9-13.

The brick-and-mortar church concept of today is a place where these two seeds, the seed of the woman and the seed of the serpent come together and mix, thus negating the necessary directive separation. Parents can only control what their children consume in the family setting, outside of this setting they are unable to effectively parent their children in selflessness and for this reason the Lord has cautioned on separation.

CHAPTER 12

THE GREAT FLOOD

"[5] And God saw that the wickedness of man was great in the earth, and that every imagination of the thoughts of his heart was only evil continually...[8] But Noah found grace in the eyes of the LORD.[9] These are the generations of Noah: Noah was a just man and perfect in his generations, and Noah walked with God.[10] And Noah begat three sons, Shem, Ham, and Japheth." Genesis 6:5, 8-10.

In a world where "self" ruled supreme, there was one man who remained selfless. Noah was said to be "perfect," for in God's estimation selflessness is perfection.

"[11] The earth also was corrupt before God, and the earth was filled with violence.[12] And God looked upon the earth, and, behold, it was corrupt; for all flesh had corrupted his way upon the earth.[13] And God said unto Noah, The end of all flesh is come before me; for the earth is filled with violence through them; and, behold, I will destroy them with the earth." Genesis 6:11-13.

The defining state of affairs before the flood was "violence," an unbridled expression of self. "[37] But as the days of Noe were, so shall also the coming of the Son of man be." Mathew 24:37. The disintegration of our civilized society has accelerated in modern times in parallel with the dissolution of the nuclear family unit. This violent trend will continue to escalate until God will once more arise and obliterate the selfish from His creation, not with water but with fire.

"[14] Make thee an ark of gopher wood; rooms shalt thou make in the ark, and shalt pitch it within and without with pitch.[15] And this is the fashion which thou shalt make it of: The length of the ark shall be three hundred cubits, the breadth of it fifty cubits, and the height of it thirty cubits [16] A window shalt thou make to the ark, and in a cubit shalt thou finish it above; and the door of the ark shalt thou set in the side thereof; with lower, second, and third stories shalt thou make it.[17] And, behold, I, even I, do bring a flood of waters upon the earth, to destroy all flesh, wherein is the breath of life, from under heaven; and every thing that is in the earth shall die." Genesis 6:14-22.**

The ark was made of "gopher wood" likely cedar or cypress. It was three stories high (52ft tall), almost 2 football fields long (515ft long) and 86ft wide – thus the ship footprint was shy of one square acre, in total, just under 3 square acres over 3 stories. A central skylight was placed in the roof of the ark for light and a door was set in its side. The ark was massive and impossible for one man to build alone. Noah likely hired contractors to help build the mammoth ship while he project-managed and financed the entire enterprise under the blessing of the Lord.

Noah was not an isolated hermit. While he remained separate from the world, not making friendships and alliances, his life was nevertheless a testament in word and in deed to the selfless character of God. Noah had been building for 20 years before his first son was born.

"[1]And the LORD said unto Noah, Come thou and all thy house into the ark; for thee have I seen righteous before me in this generation. [2] Of every clean beast thou

shalt take to thee by sevens, the male and his female: and of beasts that are not clean by two, the male and his female.[3] Of fowls also of the air by sevens, the male and the female; to keep seed alive upon the face of all the earth." Genesis 7:1-3.

Noah was instructed to bring along 7 pairs of clean animals and birds (male and female) and 2 pairs of unclean animals from every species. The distinction between clean and unclean animals was evidently well known to Noah. It was only after centuries of sin when this knowledge had been lost that God again recorded these differences by the hand of Moses in the Book of Leviticus. God directed for more clean than unclean animals to be saved to meet the food emergency, sacrificial requirements and to prevent the extinction of the species.

"[4] For yet seven days, and I will cause it to rain upon the earth forty days and forty nights; and every living substance that I have made will I destroy from off the face of the earth.[5] And Noah did according unto all that the LORD commanded him.[6] And Noah was six hundred years old when the flood of waters was upon the earth.

[7] And Noah went in, and his sons, and his wife, and his sons' wives with him, into the ark, because of the waters of the flood. [8] Of clean beasts, and of beasts that are not clean, and of fowls, and of every thing that creepeth upon the earth, [9] There went in two and two unto Noah into the ark, the male and the female, as God had commanded Noah." Genesis 7:4-9.

Seven days prior to the start of the flood, Noah and his family were permitted to enter the ark first, which was then followed by scores of animals. For seven days they were to position themselves and the animals for their long voyage to the new world, celebrating at least one Sabbath before their departure.

"[11] In the six hundredth year of Noah's life, in the second month, the seventeenth day of the month, the same day were all the fountains of the great deep broken up, and the windows of heaven were opened. [12] And the rain was upon the earth forty days and forty nights." Genesis 7: 11, 12

At the age of 600, at the time appointed, on May 17th the earth's mantle was broken open and jets of water gushed from the ground hurling rocks and trees into the air while the clouds poured rain for forty days and forty nights. There are subterranean seas located 400 miles deep within the earth's mantle that contain 3 times more water than the ocean; all this was liberated when the "fountains of the great deep" were broken open.

"[17] And the flood was forty days upon the earth; and the waters increased, and bare up the ark, and it was lift up above the earth. [18] And the waters prevailed, and were increased greatly upon the earth; and the ark went upon the face of the waters. [19] And the waters prevailed exceedingly upon the earth; and all the high hills, that were under the whole heaven, were covered. [20] Fifteen cubits upward did the waters prevail; and the mountains were covered.

[21] And all flesh died that moved upon the earth, both of fowl, and of cattle, and of beast, and of every creeping thing that creepeth upon the earth, and every man: [22] All

in whose nostrils was the breath of life, of all that was in the dry land, died.[23] And every living substance was destroyed which was upon the face of the ground, both man, and cattle, and the creeping things, and the fowl of the heaven; and they were destroyed from the earth: and Noah only remained alive, and they that were with him in the ark.[24] And the waters prevailed upon the earth an hundred and fifty days." Genesis 7:17-24.

The flood was not merely a local phenomenon in the Mesopotamian Valley but of worldwide extent. The entire planet was under water; only the inhabitants of the ark remained alive. The catastrophic effects of the flood are seen today as evidenced by the fossils of plants and animals that can be found from one end of the earth to the other. In some places these fossils can be found almost three miles deep into the earth's surface.

The worldwide distribution of these fossils and the depth of their burial is an indication not only of the universal distribution of the flood but the sheer force and terrific violence of the storm. No matter how well the ark was built it was only preserved by divine intervention.

CHAPTER 13

THE NEW WORLD

"³ And the waters returned from off the earth continually: and after the end of the hundred and fifty days the waters were abated. ⁴ And the ark rested in the seventh month, on the seventeenth day of the month, upon the mountains of Ararat.⁵ And the waters decreased continually until the tenth month: in the tenth month, on the first day of the month, were the tops of the mountains seen." Genesis 8:3-5

After almost 6 months out at sea the ark came to rest on the mountaintops of Ararat (Modern day Turkey). On the 17ᵗʰ day of the 7ᵗʰ month which would be October 17ᵗʰ assuming the months to be 30 days, the waters continued to subside until the mountaintops are visible on the 1ˢᵗ of the 10ᵗʰ month, which would be around January 1ˢᵗ.

"⁶ And it came to pass at the end of forty days, that Noah opened the window of the ark which he had made: ⁷ And he sent forth a raven, which went forth to and fro, until the waters were dried up from off the earth.

⁸ Also he sent forth a dove from him, to see if the waters were abated from off the face of the ground; ⁹ But the dove found no rest for the sole of her foot, and she returned unto him into the ark, for the waters were on the face of the whole earth: then he put forth his hand, and took her, and pulled her in unto him into the ark.

¹⁰ And he stayed yet other seven days; and again he sent forth the dove out of the ark;¹¹ And the dove came in to him in the evening; and, lo, in her mouth was an olive leaf pluckt off: so Noah knew that the waters were

abated from off the earth.[12] And he stayed yet other seven days; and sent forth the dove; which returned not again unto him any more." Genesis 8:6-12

Knowing the flight patterns of these two different birds Noah was better able to get a sense of the water's recession and the availability of dry land. The low flying, less agile dove was sent out on 3 separate occasions a week apart. On the first mission the dove returned with an empty beak, on the second it returned with an olive branch and on the third, the dove failed to return indicating there was dry ground on which it could rest.

"[13] And it came to pass in the six hundredth and first year, in the first month, the first day of the month, the waters were dried up from off the earth: and Noah removed the covering of the ark, and looked, and, behold, the face of the ground was dry." Genesis 8:13.

On April 1st at the age of 601 Noah removed the lid from the ark and he was able to see the dry ground. God had shut the door and Noah now awaited God to open the door.

"[14] And in the second month, on the seven and twentieth day of the month, was the earth dried.[15] And God spake unto Noah, saying, [16] Go forth of the ark, thou, and thy wife, and thy sons, and thy sons' wives with thee." Genesis 8:14-16.

On the 27th day of the second month, May 27th, the earth was sufficiently dry for Noah and his family to safely disembark under the direction of the Lord. Noah had been in the ark almost an exact year, the flood commencing May 17th the year before.

"¹⁸ And Noah went forth, and his sons, and his wife, and his sons' wives with him: ¹⁹ Every beast, every creeping thing, and every fowl, and whatsoever creepeth upon the earth, after their kinds, went forth out of the ark." Genesis 8:18,19.

"¹ And God blessed Noah and his sons, and said unto them, Be fruitful, and multiply, and replenish the earth.² And the fear of you and the dread of you shall be upon every beast of the earth, and upon every fowl of the air, upon all that moveth upon the earth, and upon all the fishes of the sea; into your hand are they delivered.

³ Every moving thing that liveth shall be meat for you; even as the green herb have I given you all things.⁴ But flesh with the life thereof, which is the blood thereof, shall ye not eat.⁵ And surely your blood of your lives will I require; at the hand of every beast will I require it, and at the hand of man; at the hand of every man's brother will I require the life of man." Genesis 9:1-5.

At creation God had given both men and beast a plant-based diet. Now to meet the emergency of a desolate earth, a meat-based diet, provided it was clean and without blood, was provided as a temporary measure. Man and beast had shared a close bond at creation but to protect the animal species from self-serving man and to prevent his over indulgence on an inferior food source, a fear of man was placed in the hearts of the beasts.

"⁸ And God spake unto Noah, and to his sons with him, saying, ⁹ And I, behold, I establish my covenant with you, and with your seed after you;... ¹³ I do set my bow in the cloud, and it shall be for a token of a covenant between me and the earth. ¹⁴ And it shall come to pass, when I bring a cloud over the earth, that the bow shall be seen in the cloud: [15] And I will remember my covenant, which is between me and you and every living creature of all flesh; and the waters shall no more become a flood to destroy all flesh." Genesis 9: 8, 9, 13-15.

Chronology of the Flood Genesis 7 & 8			
	Month	Day	Noah's Age
Noah Enters the ark (Gen 7: 4,7,10)	2	10	600
Beginning of the flood (Gen 7:11) - May 17th	2	17	600
Rain for 40 days (Gen 7:4,12,17)	3	27	600
The "waters prevail" another 110 days (Gen 7:24)	7	17	600
The ark rests upon Mt Ararat (Gen 8:4)- Oct 17th	7	17	600
The mountains seen (Gen 8:5)	10	1	600
The raven released forty days later (Gen 8:6)	11	11	600
Dove released the 1st time (Gen 8:8)	11	18	600
Dove released the 2nd time (Gen 8:10)	11	25	600
Dove released the 3rd time (Gen 8:12)	12	2	600
Covering removed (Gen 8:13)- May 1st	1	1	601
Noah leaves the ark (Gen 8: 14-16)- May 27th	2	27	601

The rainbow was a sign of the covenant that God would never again destroy the earth by a flood. The rainbow was the assurance that after every rainstorm there would be sunshine followed with calmness and tranquility, a reminder of the rainbow that surrounds the throne of God (Revelation 4:3). Noah was in the ark for an exact year, Noah died 350 years after the flood when he was 950 years old (Genesis 9:29).

The Two Seeds Emerge Once More

"**20 And Noah began to be an husbandman, and he planted a vineyard: 21 And he drank of the wine, and was drunken; and he was uncovered within his tent. 22 And Ham, the father of Canaan, saw the nakedness of his father, and told his two brethren without.23 And Shem and Japheth took a garment, and laid it upon both their shoulders, and went backward, and covered the nakedness of their father; and their faces were backward, and they saw not their father's nakedness.**" **Genesis 9:20-23.**

Noah and his family departed from the ark and through his three sons, Shem, Ham and Japheth the earth was again populated. In the course of time Noah planted a vineyard and became intoxicated. Ham, finding his father in a compromised state selfishly ridiculed him. The two other brothers motivated by selflessness went to preserve the honor of their father by covering him with a piece of clothing. The selfish nature of Ham was transmitted to his son Canaan who became the head of an idolatrous nation, the Canaanites.

Noah and his family arrived in the New World swept clean of sin, but the selfish human nature inherited from their first parents after their fall remained then and remains today. This tendency to selfishness will remain until Christ's returns at which time we shall be changed in a "twinkling of an eye" back to a selfless human nature as it was in Eden. Until then a selfless nature can only be maintained by a daily dying to self, in the words of Paul: "I die daily." 1 Corinthians 15:31.

"[24] And Noah awoke from his wine, and knew what his younger son had done unto him.[25] And he said, Cursed be Canaan; a servant of servants shall he be unto his brethren.[26] And he said, Blessed be the LORD God of Shem; and Canaan shall be his servant.[27] God shall enlarge Japheth, and he shall dwell in the tents of Shem; and Canaan shall be his servant. [28] And Noah lived after the flood three hundred and fifty years.[29] And all the days of Noah were nine hundred and fifty years: and he died." Genesis 9:24-29.**

These blessings and curses pronounced here were not a punitive decree by which the destiny of each son was determined. Noah knew the characters of his sons and the curses and the blessings he offered were prophetic. He gave them a glimpse into their futures, which they should form by their own choices. Both the descendants of Canaan and the descendants of Japheth were to serve the descendants of Shem. Shem had chosen the service of God and as such he was to be an inheritor of all the promises and blessings of salvation.

CHAPTER 14

BABYLON AND ITS ICONIC TOWER

"⁶And the sons of Ham; Cush, …⁸And Cush begat Nimrod: …¹⁰And the beginning of his kingdom was Babel… in the land of Shinar…" Genesis 10:6, 8, 10

The God-fearing descendants of Noah remained in the hills where the ark settled, while self-serving Ham and his descendants traveled down into the plains of Shinar in southern Mesopotamia. Mesopotamia which means "between rivers" was a geographical area between the Tigris and Euphrates, now in modern day Iraq. Here along the banks of the River Euphrates, Nimrod, the great grandson of Noah through Ham, built for themselves a mighty civilization, the Kingdom of Babylon with its iconic Tower of Babel.

The Babylonian Empire founded by King Hammurabi in the 18th century BC was the first grand scale urban development administered by a central government guided by the system of error in the form of paganism.

Mesopotamia was known as the cradle of civilizations due to its advances in agriculture, irrigation, writing, the wheel, and glass. The first form of writing was the Cuneiform script dating 3000BC.

Each succeeding civilization through the millennia; Persia, Greece, and Rome were all built upon the blueprint of Babylon: urbanization, central government and a cohesive system of error in the form of paganism. Today's legal systems and the rule of law are based on the ancient "Code of Hammurabi" written around 1750 BC on a stone cylinder. The cylinder now housed in the Louvre, is 7ft tall and is embossed with engravings of the sun god and the god of justice. The laws of Hammurabi were broad and focused on various aspects of managing an urban society and included criminal law, family law, property law and commercial law. The US Capitol has a relief portrait of Hammurabi and there are replicas of the stone cylinder in the United Nations building in New York City and the Pergamon Museum in Berlin.

King Nebuchadnezzar II (604–562 BC) reigned at the peak of the Neo-Babylonian Empire. He conquered Jerusalem and enslaved the Jews in Babylon, including the prophet Daniel. Nebuchadnezzar ordered the construction of one of the 8 main processional entrances to the inner City of Babylon, the Ishtar Gate on the north side of the city. This gate was dedicated to the goddess Ishtar. The gate was constructed using glazed brick relief with alternating rows of the god Marduk, the patron god of the city and his servant dragon Mušḫuššu who is pictured in stone relief as opening the gates to Babylon. The gate was relocated and can be seen today at the Pergamon Museum in Berlin, Germany.

"[1] And the whole earth was of one language, and of one speech …[4] And they said, Go to, let us build us a city and a tower, whose top may reach unto heaven; and let us make us a name, lest we be scattered abroad upon the face of the whole earth." Genesis 11:1, 4.

The architects were to build a "city" and a "tower" whose influence would "reach heaven." The "city" was to be a place of urbanization, the "tower," the seat of government. Its influence would "reach heaven," that is to span the entire globe. In the name "Babel", "bab" means gate and "el" means "god" thus the "gateway to the gods." Paganism is the religion of self-sufficiency and independence of God.

The intent of Satan was to build himself a rival kingdom to that of God using these men as his agents. God's seat of selfless government is in the heavenly Jerusalem. Satan's seat of self-serving government would initially be in ancient Babylon and later it would grow and overspread the whole earth as mystical Babylon of Revelation – a global Babylon in principle and system.

"4 That thou shalt take up this proverb against the king of Babylon, and say, How hath the oppressor ceased! the golden city ceased! 12 How art thou fallen from heaven, O Lucifer, son of the morning! how art thou cut down to the ground, which didst weaken the nations!13 For thou hast said in thine heart, I will ascend into heaven, I will exalt my throne above the stars of God: I will sit also upon the mount of the congregation, in the sides of the north:14 I will ascend above the heights of the clouds; I will be like the most High.15 Yet thou shalt be brought down to hell, to the sides of the pit." Isaiah 14:4,12-14.

The scripture uses the imagery of Lucifer as the King of Babylon who tried to unseat his maker but was cast out. Instead of setting his intended throne in the new Jerusalem he is forced to establish his throne on earth in Babylon as the King of Babylon.

"5 And the LORD came down to see the city and the tower, which the children of men builded. 6 And the LORD said, Behold, the people is one, and they have all one language; and this they begin to do: and now nothing will be restrained from them, which they have

imagined to do. [7] Go to, let us go down, and there confound their language, that they may not understand one another's speech.

[8] So the LORD scattered them abroad from thence upon the face of all the earth: and they left off to build the city. [9] Therefore is the name of it called Babel; because the LORD did there confound the language of all the earth: and from thence did the LORD scatter them abroad upon the face of all the earth." Genesis 11:5-9.

The Lord's direction in Eden was for mankind to spread out over the earth and multiply that each nuclear family unit might have their own land where they could function as a school and a church under the government of God. The system of Babylon defied the divine will by urbanizing mankind under central government. The Lord confused the language of the people in ancient Babylon to slow the inevitable results of urbanization as seen in the great cities of today: fracturing of the nuclear family unit, overcrowding, unemployment, homelessness, poverty, and spiraling crime.

Babylon the Great

"5 And upon her forehead was a name written, MYSTERY, BABYLON THE GREAT, THE MOTHER OF HARLOTS AND ABOMINATIONS OF THE EARTH. [18] And the woman which thou sawest is that great city, which reigneth over the kings of the earth." Revelation 17: 5,18

The Book of Revelation brings to view Satan's rival government as mystical Babylon. This government consists of three components (Revelation 16:19): the Dragon, the Beast and the False Prophet. The Dragon represents the Devil himself (Revelation 12:9) as the mastermind of this government. The Beast represents the system of human government (Revelation 13:1-10) and its urbanized society (Revelation 17:18).

The False Prophet (Revelation 19:20), also known as the "lamb like beast that speaks as a dragon" (Revelation 13:11-18), represents the system of error. These three components of Global Babylon are the counterfeit to the government of God.

	God's Government	Satan's Government
Home Base	New Jerusalem	Global Babylon
Member 1	God the Father (7)	The Dragon, Devil (6)
Member 2	God the Son (7)	The Beast, System of Human Government (6)
Member 3	God the Holy Spirit (7)	False Prophet, System of Error (6)
Society/Image	Selfless	Self-serving
Number of his name	777	666

Ancient Babylon owed its success to the "system of human government" and its cohesive "system of error." This system of error involves falsehood at every level whether it be of a religious nature or a false narrative of sorts. The system of error is always coupled with a campaign of fear, for fear is of the Devil. A common belief system based upon a system of error is the mortar that held the bricks of society in cohesion and submission to the system of government.

In Revelation 18, Satan's government is personified as a global prostitute who knows no loyalty and no greater good than the service of self. This system of government was transmitted from one civilization to the next right down to our own modern time. Every nation on earth today has a well-developed system of government with a "cabinet" overseeing every aspect of human life.

A cabinet generally consists of secretaries of the treasury, defense, interior, agriculture, commerce, labor, health and human services, urban development, transportation, energy, education, homeland security, environmental protection, and intelligence. Each of these secretaries create a spin that causes the people to buy into their narrative or suffer its restrictions.

In ancient Rome failing to worship according to the state sanctioned religion of paganism led to death under emperors Nero and Diocletian. In the Holy Roman Empire failing to worship according to the state religion of Catholicism led to persecution and death at the stake.

In modern times the campaign of fear has involved the COVID 19 pandemic and the loss of employment for failing to comply with the government vaccine mandates. In the near future there will be consequences for violating carbon emission standards under the threat of the looming "cataclysm" of global warming. With 59% of the world's population urbanized, the blueprint of ancient Babylon is fast becoming a Global Babylon.

Every aspect of our urbanized existence comes under government regulation which is complicit in fracturing the nuclear family unit. Urbanized parents go to work leaving their children to be educated by strangers in the service of self, thus negating the protective provisions of separation. The disposition of the child quickly changes after they enter school where they learn selfishness and defiance from their peers. Without parental guidance children often develop anxiety and emotional issues who later go on to self-medicate using drugs and alcohol.

Life in the cities where space is limited leaves children after school and on weekends to inactivity, social media, and delinquency. The relaxing scenes of nature are lost in the concrete city leading to increased anxiety. As employment is limited, overcrowding, homelessness and drugs have become endemic. High taxation and corporate greed lead to a low quality of life for the masses as parents are enslaved by debt, ever working and never able to get ahead. Once parents are old and gray and unable to pay their property taxes, they lose their life's work to the government and are then retired to an old age home to die, and so the whore of Babylon is serviced and the cycle repeats.

Under the divine plan the nuclear family unit will thrive in a "country living" paradigm: working together, eating together, playing together, learning together, laughing together, and worshiping together in selflessness. In the country setting children learn the importance of co-operation with the invaluable lessons of industry, reliability, and accountability. Family cohesion leads to mental stability. Working in nature brings peace of mind.

The Amish way of life is the closest approximation to the divine plan. Physical and mental health issues are largely unseen amongst the Amish. Crime and divorce are almost unheard of. The highest ideal of this community is to reflect the selfless image of God and the greatest enjoyment is the social transactions within the family.

The great object of the gospel is the restoration of the nuclear family unit: "[5] Behold, I will send you Elijah the prophet before the coming of the great and dreadful day of the LORD:[6] And he shall turn the heart of the fathers to the children, and the heart of the children to their fathers,..." Malachi 4:5,6.

"[2] And he cried mightily with a strong voice, saying, Babylon the great is fallen, is fallen, [4] ...Come out of her, my people, that ye be not partakers of her sins, and that ye receive not of her plagues." Revelation 18:2, 4.

God is calling His people out of global Babylon for a life of country living. In the country setting, separated from those who live to the service of self, the mind can be sanitized from the theories of pagan Christianity. Here the nuclear family unit can once again become a church and a school. Under the influence of the Holy Spirit the character can be changed to reflect the selfless image of God.

Volume two of this series documents Abraham's journey as God leads him and his family out of ancient Babylon. His journey is not merely a "moral" story, but it is the blueprint journey for spiritual Jews today who are seeking to leave Global Babylon behind.

SECTION IV
ABRAHAM AND
ISAAC

CHAPTER 15

LEAVING BABYLON

"²⁷ Now these are the generations of Terah: Terah begat Abram, Nahor, and Haran; and Haran begat Lot.²⁸ And Haran died before his father Terah in the land of his nativity, in Ur of the Chaldees...³¹ And Terah took Abram his son, and Lot the son of Haran his son's son, and Sarai his daughter in law, his son Abram's wife; and they went forth with them from Ur of the Chaldees, to go into the land of Canaan; and they came unto Haran, and dwelt there.³² And the days of Terah were two hundred and five years: and Terah died in Haran."
Genesis 11:27-32

The call from God to separate from the world now comes to the House of Terah, a direct descendant of Noah (Genesis 11:10-26). Terah took his son Abram, Abram's wife Sarai and his grandson Lot and departed from Ur in Lower Mesopotamia, just south of the City of Babylon in the fertile valley between the Tigris and Euphrates Rivers, now modern-day Iraq.

The call was to leave this well civilized area for the remote, thick wooded mountains in Canaan which were inhabited by poorly civilized tribes, some 1500 miles away. Their first stop was in the City of Haran in Upper Mesopotamia, just north of Babylon about 600 miles away. The family undoubtedly passed through Babylon witnessing its iconic tower built as a monument of self-serving.

Terah and his family were called to be separate from the world so that their characters might be purified from self-serving. While in Haran, Terah died at the age of 205.

Abram lived about 450 years after the flood and 2,107 years after creation.

"¹Now the LORD had said unto Abram, Get thee out of thy country, and from thy kindred, and from thy father's house, unto a land that I will shew thee:² And I will make of thee a great nation, and I will bless thee, and make thy name great; and thou shalt be a blessing:³ And I will bless them that bless thee, and curse him that curseth thee: and in thee shall all families of the earth be blessed.

⁴ So Abram departed, as the LORD had spoken unto him; and Lot went with him: and Abram was seventy and five years old when he departed out of Haran.⁵ And Abram took Sarai his wife, and Lot his brother's son, and all their substance that they had gathered, and the souls that they had gotten in Haran; and they went forth to go into the land of Canaan; and into the land of Canaan they came." Genesis 12:1-5.

Following the death of Terah, God now calls Abram, now 75 years old, to the onward journey to a land of inheritance where Abram and his descendants, separate from idolatry, could become a selfless people reflecting the image of God and through whom the promised Messiah would come. "⁸ By faith Abraham, when he was called to go out into a place which he should after receive for an inheritance, obeyed; and he went out, not knowing whither he went…" Hebrews 11:8.

"⁵…and into the land of Canaan they came. ⁶ And Abram passed through the land unto the place of Sichem, unto the plain of Moreh. And the Canaanite was then in the land. ⁷ And the LORD appeared unto Abram,

and said, Unto thy seed will I give this land: and there builded he an altar unto the LORD, who appeared unto him." Genesis 12:5-7.

After an approximate 450-mile journey from Haran, Abram arrived in Canaan only to find it drought stricken and inhabited by Canaanites. The land known as Canaan was situated in the territory of the southern Levant, which today encompasses Israel, Gaza, the West Bank, Jordan, and the southern portions of Syria and Lebanon. God now appears to Abram a third time, the first though in Canaan, with words of encouragement repeating the promise.

"[10] And there was a famine in the land: and Abram went down into Egypt to sojourn there; for the famine was grievous in the land...." Genesis 12:10.

Due to the drought Abram was now forced into Egypt for a time to obtain provisions. Abram's wife was a beautiful woman, and the Egyptians would not regard his life to obtain her, so he declared Sarai to be his sister, which was true in part since she was his half-sister. Pharaoh, hearing of Sarai's beauty, thought to take her to be his wife, but the Lord plagued Pharaoh and he released Sarai. In this experience Abram doubted God's protective power and he resorted to strategy to preserve himself as though God who had led him so far would not have preserved him. Despite Abram's lack of trust, the Lord in his love and mercy shielded His children.

CHAPTER 16

ABRAM PAYS TITHE TO MELCHISEDEC

"[7] And there was a strife between the herdmen of Abram's cattle and the herdmen of Lot's cattle: and the Canaanite and the Perizzite dwelled then in the land. [8] And Abram said unto Lot, Let there be no strife, I pray thee, between me and thee, and between my herdmen and thy herdmen; for we be brethren. [9] Is not the whole land before thee? separate thyself, I pray thee, from me: if thou wilt take the left hand, then I will go to the right; or if thou depart to the right hand, then I will go to the left.

[10] And Lot lifted up his eyes, and beheld all the plain of Jordan, that it was well watered every where, before the LORD destroyed Sodom and Gomorrah, even as the garden of the LORD, like the land of Egypt, as thou comest unto Zoar. [11] Then Lot chose him all the plain of Jordan.... [12] Abram dwelled in the land of Canaan, and Lot dwelled in the cities of the plain, and pitched his tent toward Sodom. [13] But the men of Sodom were wicked and sinners before the LORD exceedingly." Genesis 13: 7-12.

Self-serving disagreements between the herdsman was driving the two families apart and they decided to part ways. Abram, to whom the land was promised selflessly offered his nephew the best of the land. Lot chose the beautiful and well-watered plains of Jordan which was also home to the cities of Sodom and Gomorrah.

"[14] And the LORD said unto Abram, after that Lot was separated from him, Lift up now thine eyes, and look from the place where thou art northward, and southward, and eastward, and westward: [15] For all the land which thou seest, to thee will I give it, and to thy seed for ever. [16] And I will make thy seed as the dust of the earth: so that if a man can number the dust of the earth, then shall thy seed also be numbered. [17] Arise, walk through the land in the length of it and in the breadth of it; for I will give it unto thee." Genesis 13:14-17

To cheer His friend after Lot's departure, the Lord now reminds Abram of the promises and his great calling. This is the fourth occasion in which the Lord spoke to Abram. Each of these occasions marked a crisis in his life and the promises were given to renew and strengthen his faith in Him who knows all and sees all.

"[8] And there went out the king of Sodom, and the king of Gomorrah, and the king of Admah, and the king of Zeboiim, and the king of Bela (the same is Zoar;) and they joined battle with them in the vale of Siddim;...[12] And they took Lot, Abram's brother's son, who dwelt in Sodom, and his goods, and departed. [13] And there came one that had escaped, and told Abram the Hebrew; for he dwelt in the plain of Mamre the Amorite, brother of Eshcol, and brother of Aner: and these were confederate with Abram." Genesis 14: 8, 12, 13

Lot had settled in Sodom, one of five main cities in the valley that paid taxes to Chedorlaomer, King of Elam. The kings of these cities now rebelled leading to an armed conflict in which Lot was captured. A fugitive who escaped "told Abram the Hebrew" that Lot had been captured. Abram immediately gathered his forces, which included

318 men from his own household. Dividing his forces into groups, Abram attacked the powerful army from different directions crushing the army and rescuing Lot (Genesis 14: 13-16).

This is the first time that Abram is referred to as the Hebrew, which means one who is "traveling through." That is one who does not participate in the self-serving social, cultural, and political fabric of the day. The Apostle Paul in Hebrews references this experience and the experiences of all God's people as they separate from a life of self-serving

"[13] These all died in faith, not having received the promises, but having seen them afar off, and were persuaded of them, and embraced them, and confessed that they were strangers and pilgrims on the earth. [14] For they that say such things declare plainly that they seek a country. [15] And truly, if they had been mindful of that country from whence they came out, they might have had opportunity to have returned. [16] But now they desire a better country, that is, an heavenly: wherefore God is not ashamed to be called their God: for he hath prepared for them a city." Hebrews 11:13-16.

"[17] And the king of Sodom went out to meet him after his return from the slaughter of Chedorlaomer, and of the kings that were with him, at the valley of Shaveh, which is the king's dale. [18] And Melchizedek king of Salem brought forth bread and wine: and he was the priest of the most high God. [19] And he blessed him, and said, Blessed be Abram of the most high God, possessor of heaven and earth: [20] And blessed be the most high God, which hath delivered thine enemies into thy hand. And he gave him tithes of all." Genesis 14:17-20.

Melchizedek, King of Salem, now joins with the king of Sodom in welcoming Abram back from the conflict. In the days of Abram, Jerusalem was known as Salem, which means "peace" and Melchizedek means "King of Righteousness" (Hebrews 7:1,2). This is the first introduction of Melchizedek in the Old Testament who is described as both a king and a priest. The word "priest" implies that there must have existed a regularly constituted form of sacrificial worship. This shows despite the wickedness of the Canaanites the Lord still had his faithful ones scattered throughout the region bearing testimony to His name.

Paul in the Book of Hebrews contrasts the Levitical Priesthood that ministered in the earthly sanctuary with Christ's Priesthood, after the order of Melchizedek, who ministers as High Priest in the heavenly sanctuary. This is also the first mention of tithing. By returning to God a tenth of one's earnings it shows that the believer recognizes God's ownership over all property and that we are merely stewards upon this earth. The system of tithe and Christ's Priesthood after the order of Melchizedek is discussed in depth in the Book of Exodus.

CHAPTER 17

EGYPTIAN BONDAGE PREDICTED

"[1]After these things the word of the LORD came unto Abram in a vision, saying, Fear not, Abram: I am thy shield, and thy exceeding great reward.[2] And Abram said, LORD God, what wilt thou give me, seeing I go childless, and the steward of my house is this Eliezer of Damascus? [3] And Abram said, Behold, to me thou hast given no seed: and, lo, one born in my house is mine heir.

[4] And, behold, the word of the LORD came unto him, saying, This shall not be thine heir; but he that shall come forth out of thine own bowels shall be thine heir.[5] And he brought him forth abroad, and said, Look now toward heaven, and tell the stars, if thou be able to number them: and he said unto him, So shall thy seed be.[6] And he believed in the LORD; and he counted it to him for righteousness.[7] And he said unto him, I am the LORD that brought thee out of Ur of the Chaldees, to give thee this land to inherit it...." Genesis 15: 1-7.

This is the fifth revelation of God to Abram and comes at a distinct turning point in Abram's life. Advancing in years he still was without an heir. Abram now proposed that he might adopt his servant Eliezer to be his heir. God directs him to the stars of heaven, the same power that spoke the stars into existence was able to speak life to the barren bodies of Abram and his wife.

"[8] And he said, LORD God, whereby shall I know that I shall inherit it?[9] And he said unto him, Take me an heifer of three years old, and a she goat of three years old, and a ram of three years old, and a turtledove, and a young pigeon.[10] And he took unto him all these, and divided them in the midst, and laid each piece one against another: but the birds divided he not.[11] And when the fowls came down upon the carcases, Abram drove them away.[12] And when the sun was going down, a deep sleep fell upon Abram; and, lo, an horror of great darkness fell upon him." Genesis 15:8-12.

God now enters a covenant with Abram in a ceremony that was customary in ancient times. Abram was to slaughter three animals and divide their bodies in half. The birds were killed but not divided. The animal halves were placed on either side of the walkway so that each of the parties who entered the covenant were to walk between the two halves, the bodies of the slain bearing record of the covenant. Whoever would break such a contract would be made like these slain animals. After Abram fell asleep, he saw a burning lamp the symbols of the divine presence pass between the divided parts thus confirming the covenant.

"[12] And when the sun was going down, a deep sleep fell upon Abram; and, lo, an horror of great darkness fell upon him. [13] And he said unto Abram, Know of a surety that thy seed shall be a stranger in a land that is not theirs, and shall serve them; and they shall afflict them four hundred years; [14] And also that nation, whom they shall serve, will I judge: and afterward shall they come out with great substance. [15] And thou shalt go to thy fathers in peace; thou shalt be buried in a good old age." Genesis 15:12-15.

It was here revealed that his descendants would be persecuted and enslaved in Egypt for 400 years before inheriting the land of Canaan. The 400-year clock would begin to tick when Isaac was "persecuted" by Ishmael. Paul, however, in Galatians 3:16 speaks of their stay as 430 years but he includes the time from Abram's original call to leave Haran to the birth of Isaac, which was 30 years.

"¹⁶ But in the fourth generation they shall come hither again: for the iniquity of the Amorites is not yet full." Genesis 15:16.

In the "fourth generation" the Israelites would leave Egypt. The length of a generation cannot be assumed to be 100 years but is rather determined by the offspring, thus the fourth generation would be the lifetime of a great-great grandson. That is one generation went into Egypt, two generations dwelt in Egypt and a fourth generation came out. Caleb for example who came out of Egypt was the fourth generation from Judah who went into Egypt. (1 Chronicles 2:3-5,18). Moses who came out of Egypt was the fourth generation from Levi who went into Egypt (Exodus 6:16-20).

If the total time between the given promise and the Exodus were 430 years and two generations spent their time in Egypt, then their total time in Egypt as slaves would have been approximately 215 years. We can therefore calculate that from creation to the flood was 1656 years, from the flood to Abram was 450 years and from Abram to the Exodus was 430 years. Thus, the people of Israel left Egypt approximately 2,536 years after creation.

There are two reasons for the delay in the divine promise. Firstly, Abram's seed would need to multiply to become a great nation and secondly, the Amorites had not reached their full measure of iniquity; "for the iniquity of the

131

Amorites is not yet full." The Amorites were the most powerful of the Canaanite tribes and were wicked beyond imagination. Nevertheless, grace was to be extended to them that they might repent. Thus, the Hebrews were not ready to possess the land nor was God ready to disinherit the Amorites. And here in is the mercy and justice of God displayed.

CHAPTER 18

ISHMAEL, THE PLAN OF MAN

"¹ Now Sarai Abram's wife bare him no children: and she had an handmaid, an Egyptian, whose name was Hagar. ² And Sarai said unto Abram, Behold now, the LORD hath restrained me from bearing: I pray thee, go in unto my maid; it may be that I may obtain children by her. And Abram hearkened to the voice of Sarai.

³ And Sarai Abram's wife took Hagar her maid the Egyptian, after Abram had dwelt ten years in the land of Canaan, and gave her to her husband Abram to be his wife. ⁴ And he went in unto Hagar, and she conceived: and when she saw that she had conceived, her mistress was despised in her eyes." Genesis 16:1-4.

Abram was 75 years old when he received the call from God to depart from Haran. After living in Canaan for 10 years now at the age of 85 Abram and Sarai become restless. They decide that the plan of God required some human intervention that it might be realized and accordingly Abram took Hagar the Egyptian servant of Sarai, to be his wife. Polygamy was never within the divine plan but having lived amongst idolaters for so long Abram had lost sight of the divine will and in some way justified his actions of taking a second wife in order that he might obtain the blessing.

"⁵ And Sarai said unto Abram, My wrong be upon thee: I have given my maid into thy bosom; and when she saw that she had conceived, I was despised in her eyes: the LORD judge between me and thee.⁶ But Abram said unto Sarai, Behold, thy maid is in thine hand; do to her as it pleaseth thee. And when Sarai dealt hardly with her, she fled from her face." Genesis 16: 5, 6

Having conceived, Hagar now becomes proud and boastful. Sarai feeling marginalized complains to Abram who tells her, without consulting God, to solve the situation as she saw fit. Sarai evidently put her in her place, Hagar feeling hurt and mistreated now flees into the wilderness.

"[7] And the angel of the LORD found her by a fountain of water in the wilderness, by the fountain in the way to Shur. [8] And he said, Hagar, Sarai's maid, whence camest thou? and whither wilt thou go? And she said, I flee from the face of my mistress Sarai. [9] And the angel of the LORD said unto her, Return to thy mistress, and submit thyself under her hands. [10] And the angel of the LORD said unto her, I will multiply thy seed exceedingly, that it shall not be numbered for multitude." Genesis 16:7-10.

The "angel of the LORD," our precious Savior now appears to Hagar and addresses her not as Abram's wife but as "Sarai's maid," indicating that this union and plan was not recognized by God. The Lord instructs Hagar to return and submit herself to Sarai and promises her that her offspring too would become a great nation. Although her son was not to be the son of the divine plan, he would nevertheless share in the promises made to Abram.

"[11] And the angel of the LORD said unto her, Behold, thou art with child, and shalt bear a son, and shalt call his name Ishmael; because the LORD hath heard thy affliction.[12] And he will be a wild man; his hand will be against every man, and every man's hand against him; and he shall dwell in the presence of all his brethren."

Genesis 16:11, 12.

The Lord declares her son to be called "Ishmael," meaning "God shall hear" a reminder to her of the Lord's care over her during this time of trial. Of Ishmael it is said that he would be "a wild man," a description of the Bedouins love of freedom. It is also declared "his hand shall be against every man," an indication of his untamed confrontational nature, as evidenced by the continual conflicts in the Middle East.

It was Ishmaels own nature that disqualified him from being the predecessor of the Messiah. God had brought Abram and Sarai together KNOWING that their child would be of the nature worthy of the Messiah. It's for this reason it is important to walk within the divine plan because God knows all and sees all. More than just eye color and hair color are transmitted by genes, nature and temperament are also strongly encoded genetically. Had a union between Abram and Hagar produced such an heir, God would have brought these together in His own time. Abram tried to make his plan God's plan; the result was only heartache. God allows His children to chart their own course with the inevitable consequences of cause and effect when they choose to go against His protective & selfless will.

CHAPTER 19

ISAAC, THE PLAN OF GOD

"¹And when Abram was ninety years old and nine, the LORD appeared to Abram, and said unto him, I am the Almighty God; walk before me, and be thou perfect." Genesis 17:1

Abram was now 99 years old, and Ishmael was around 13 when God called Abram to re-affirm his walk in selflessness and further outlining this walk with a physical sign of the covenant and commemorative change in name.

"² And I will make my covenant between me and thee, and will multiply thee exceedingly.³ And Abram fell on his face: and God talked with him, saying,⁴ As for me, behold, my covenant is with thee, and thou shalt be a father of many nations.⁵ Neither shall thy name any more be called Abram, but thy name shall be Abraham; for a father of many nations have I made thee.

⁶ And I will make thee exceeding fruitful, and I will make nations of thee, and kings shall come out of thee.⁷ And I will establish my covenant between me and thee and thy seed after thee in their generations for an everlasting covenant, to be a God unto thee, and to thy seed after thee.⁸ And I will give unto thee, and to thy seed after thee, the land wherein thou art a stranger, all the land of Canaan, for an everlasting possession; and I will be their God." Genesis 17:2-8.

The Covenant of Salvation established with Adam was now extended to Abram. The Eden Promise paraphrasing: "I will put enmity between thee **(you the devil)** and the woman **(Eve),** and between thy seed **(the followers of Satan)** and her seed **(Eve's descendants)**; it **(the Messiah, the pre-eminent "seed" Galatians 3:16)** shall bruise thy head, and thou shalt bruise his heel." Genesis 3:15.

The seed of the woman was to be continued through Abram who would be the forerunner of the Messiah. The extension of the covenant from Adam to Abram was to be commemorated by a change of name and the ritual of circumcision. God assures Abram that he is to be the father of many nations and as such his name was to be changed from Abram "exalted father" to Abraham "father of a great number." This change indicated that the fulfillment of this promise was to be imminent.

"[9] And God said unto Abraham, Thou shalt keep my covenant therefore, thou, and thy seed after thee in their generations.[10] This is my covenant, which ye shall keep, between me and you and thy seed after thee; Every man child among you shall be circumcised.[11] And ye shall circumcise the flesh of your foreskin; and it shall be a token of the covenant betwixt me and you.

[12] And he that is eight days old shall be circumcised among you, every man child in your generations, he that is born in the house, or bought with money of any stranger, which is not of thy seed.[13] He that is born in thy house, and he that is bought with thy money, must needs be circumcised: and my covenant shall be in your flesh for an everlasting covenant.[14] And the uncircumcised man child whose flesh of his foreskin is not circumcised, that soul shall be cut off from his people; he hath broken my covenant." Genesis 17:9-14

The sign of the covenant through all generations was to be on the very organ of generation and was to be performed by every father as a promise and commitment to raise their sons within the covenant. Any male who would join Abraham's household seeking to be partakers of the covenant of salvation were to be circumcised. Since the covenant was given in Eden, repeated to Abraham, and confirmed at the cross, circumcision remains a requirement in perpetuity. Those who refused the ritual were excluded from the Covenant of Salvation.

"[15] And God said unto Abraham, As for Sarai thy wife, thou shalt not call her name Sarai, but Sarah shall her name be.[16] And I will bless her, and give thee a son also of her: yea, I will bless her, and she shall be a mother of nations; kings of people shall be of her.[17] Then Abraham fell upon his face, and laughed, and said in his heart, Shall a child be born unto him that is an hundred years old? and shall Sarah, that is ninety years old, bear?" Genesis 17:15-17.

Sarai is now mentioned for the first time as the one specifically to bear the son of promise. As the fulfillment was imminent her name was also changed to reflect the experience. Her name was changed from Sarai meaning "my princess" to Sarah "a princess." Formerly she had been Abraham's princess, now she was to be formerly recognized as the princess and progenitor of the entire nation. She belonged now not only to Abraham but to her descendants also.

"[18] And Abraham said unto God, O that Ishmael might live before thee![19] And God said, Sarah thy wife shall bear thee a son indeed; and thou shalt call his name

138

Isaac: and I will establish my covenant with him for an everlasting covenant, and with his seed after him.[20] And as for Ishmael, I have heard thee: Behold, I have blessed him, and will make him fruitful, and will multiply him exceedingly; twelve princes shall he beget, and I will make him a great nation.[21] But my covenant will I establish with Isaac, which Sarah shall bear unto thee at this set time in the next year.[22] And he left off talking with him, and God went up from Abraham." Genesis 17:18-22.

The fatherly heart of Abraham now pleads for his beloved son Ishmael that he be not excluded. Ishmael was excluded because he was the result of human devising and possessed a turbulent nature, yet he would be blessed with 12 sons and become the father of a great nation. While Ishmael could participate in the covenant blessings, in a general sense, it would however be the offspring of Isaac that would possess the Promised Land and through whom the Messiah would come.

"[23] And Abraham took Ishmael his son, and all that were born in his house, and all that were bought with his money, every male among the men of Abraham's house; and circumcised the flesh of their foreskin in the selfsame day, as God had said unto him.

[24] And Abraham was ninety years old and nine, when he was circumcised in the flesh of his foreskin.[25] And Ishmael his son was thirteen years old, when he was circumcised in the flesh of his foreskin.[26] In the selfsame day was Abraham circumcised, and Ishmael his son.[27] And all the men of his house, born in the house, and bought with money of the stranger, were

circumcised with him." Genesis 17: 23-27.

Sarah's Laughter

"[1] And the LORD appeared unto him in the plains of Mamre: and he sat in the tent door in the heat of the day; [2] And he lift up his eyes and looked, and, lo, three men stood by him: and when he saw them, he ran to meet them from the tent door, and bowed himself toward the ground,

[3] And said, My Lord, if now I have found favour in thy sight, pass not away, I pray thee, from thy servant: [4] Let a little water, I pray you, be fetched, and wash your feet, and rest yourselves under the tree:[5] And I will fetch a morsel of bread, and comfort ye your hearts; after that ye shall pass on:

...[8] And he took butter, and milk, and the calf which he had dressed, and set it before them; and he stood by them under the tree, and they did eat.

[9] And they said unto him, Where is Sarah thy wife? And he said, Behold, in the tent.[10] And he said, I will certainly return unto thee according to the time of life; and, lo, Sarah thy wife shall have a son. And Sarah heard it in the tent door, which was behind him.[11] Now Abraham and Sarah were old and well stricken in age; and it ceased to be with Sarah after the manner of women.[12] Therefore Sarah laughed within herself, saying, After I am waxed old shall I have pleasure, my lord being old also?

[13] And the LORD said unto Abraham, Wherefore did Sarah laugh, saying, Shall I of a surety bear a child,

which am old? [14] Is any thing too hard for the LORD? At the time appointed I will return unto thee, according to the time of life, and Sarah shall have a son.[15] Then Sarah denied, saying, I laughed not; for she was afraid. And he said, Nay; but thou didst laugh.[16] And the men rose up from thence, and looked toward Sodom: and Abraham went with them to bring them on the way." Genesis 18:1-5, 8-16.

Abraham was a hospitable man and invited what appeared to be three strangers in for some refreshments, but it was soon revealed that these were heavenly beings in human form. One was the Lord the other two were angels. Abraham had addressed the one as "Lord" from the word "adonai" meaning sir, but the divine record declares this to be the LORD (YHWH). This was not God the Father, since no man has seen the Father (John 1:18), but it was Christ, the messenger of the LORD.

While "messenger" is not emphatically stated it is implied by the fact He was bringing a message of the good news of Sarah's conception. Sarah laughed at the notion given her age but when her faith was questioned, she denied it out of fear.

The Birth of Isaac

"[1] And the LORD visited Sarah as he had said, and the LORD did unto Sarah as he had spoken. [2] For Sarah conceived, and bare Abraham a son in his old age, at the set time of which God had spoken to him. [3] And Abraham called the name of his son that was born unto him, whom Sarah bare to him, Isaac.

^{4} And Abraham circumcised his son Isaac being eight days old, as God had commanded him. ^{5} And Abraham was an hundred years old, when his son Isaac was born unto him. ^{6} And Sarah said, God hath made me to laugh, so that all that hear will laugh with me. ^{7} And she said, Who would have said unto Abraham, that Sarah should have given children suck? for I have born him a son in his old age." Genesis 21:1-7.

"God hath made me to laugh..." Sarah's giggle a year previously had reflected a weakened faith but now she laughed with joy. The loyalty of this family of two through the long years of delay and disappointment was now rewarded. The birth of Isaac was a token that the entire promise was to be fulfilled; the promise of the Messiah, the spreading of the gospel to all nations and the eternal home in the heavenly Canaan was also to be realized.

Ishmael Banished

"^{8} And the child grew, and was weaned: and Abraham made a great feast the same day that Isaac was weaned.^{9} And Sarah saw the son of Hagar the Egyptian, which she had born unto Abraham, mocking. ^{10} Wherefore she said unto Abraham, Cast out this bondwoman and her son: for the son of this bondwoman shall not be heir with my son, even with Isaac. ^{11} And the thing was very grievous in Abraham's sight because of his son." Genesis 21:8-11.

Weaning in the oriental custom occurred around three years of age. Ishmael was 14 when Isaac was born thus, he was approximately 17 years old when Isaac was weaned. Until the birth of Isaac, Ishmael had certainly regarded himself as his father's heir. The weaning feast made it clear to him that this was not to be the case. Ishmael with jealousy now taunted Isaac as being the younger, indirectly saying he would not receive the birthright. Paul declares this taunting to be "persecution." Galatians 4:29. Sarah was enraged and called upon her husband to send both Hagar and Ishmael away.

"12 And God said unto Abraham, Let it not be grievous in thy sight because of the lad, and because of thy bondwoman; in all that Sarah hath said unto thee, hearken unto her voice; for in Isaac shall thy seed be called. 13 And also of the son of the bondwoman will I make a nation, because he is thy seed. 14 And Abraham rose up early in the morning, and took bread, and a bottle of water, and gave it unto Hagar, putting it on her shoulder, and the child, and sent her away: and she departed, and wandered in the wilderness of Beersheba." Genesis 21:12-14.

God had never recognized the marriage between Abraham and Hagar, and to God Hagar always remained "the bondwoman." To preserve the selfless fabric of the nuclear family unit, Hagar and Ishmael were to be sent away. This was certainly a heart-rending experience for Abraham, but this was the result of trusting to the plan of man by taking to himself his servant for a wife. The restoration of the family unit as a school and church was to begin with Abraham and Sarah. A blended family with two contending wives and children would only frustrate God's ideal for the family.

Hagar and Ishmael were now given "bread and a bottle" a collective term for a meal. The fond father surely packed ample provisions for his son to make a long journey most likely back to their native Egypt. The scriptures declare that they began to "wander" indicating they lost their way and for this reason the provisions of food and water ran out.

"**15 And the water was spent in the bottle, and she cast the child under one of the shrubs. 16 And she went, and sat her down over against him a good way off, as it were a bowshot: for she said, Let me not see the death of the child. And she sat over against him, and lift up her voice, and wept. 17 And God heard the voice of the lad; and the angel of God called to Hagar out of heaven, and said unto her, What aileth thee, Hagar? fear not; for God hath heard the voice of the lad where he is. 18 Arise, lift up the lad, and hold him in thine hand; for I will make him a great nation.**

19 And God opened her eyes, and she saw a well of water; and she went, and filled the bottle with water, and gave the lad drink. 20 And God was with the lad; and he grew, and dwelt in the wilderness, and became an archer. 21 And he dwelt in the wilderness of Paran: and his mother took him a wife out of the land of Egypt."
Genesis 21:15-21.

The "angel of the LORD," our merciful Savior, again calls out to her, encouraging her and reminding her of the promise that Ishmael would become a great nation. The Lord then directs her to a nearby well and they were preserved. The years rolled on and Ishmael remained in the wilderness of Paran, the modern-day Arabian Peninsula becoming a mighty nation through his twelve sons.

CHAPTER 20

PAUL'S ANALOGY OF THE TWO COVENANTS

"**22 For it is written, that Abraham had two sons, the one by a bondmaid, the other by a freewoman. 23 But he who was of the bondwoman was born after the flesh; but he of the freewoman was by promise" Galatians 4:22, 23.**

Abraham had two sons, Ishmael from his servant Hagar, a relationship of human devising, and a son Isaac from his barren wife, conceived by divine intervention.

"**24 Which things are an allegory: for these are the two covenants; the one from the mount Sinai, which gendereth to bondage, which is Agar.25 For this Agar is mount Sinai in Arabia, and answereth to Jerusalem which now is, and is in bondage with her children.26 But Jerusalem which is above is free, which is the mother of us all." Galatians 4:24-26**

Paul creates an analogy, he compares Ishmael to the Old Covenant and Isaac to the New Covenant, that he might explain the differences between righteousness by works and righteousness by faith.

The status of the covenant is deemed "old" or "new" depending on the date of certification in blood. The "New Covenant" was given in Eden, repeated to Abraham, and certified on Calvary; hence it is said to be "new" even though it predated the "Old Covenant" which was both given and certified at Sinai with the blood of an animal. The "Old Covenant" was given in the interim until Christ should

145

come and seal the covenant with His blood and the subsequent outpouring of the Holy Spirit.

"27 For it is written, Rejoice, thou barren that bearest not; break forth and cry, thou that travailest not: for the desolate hath many more children than she which hath an husband." Galatians 4:27

Here however, Paul quotes from Isaiah 54:1 and applies it to his analogy. Isaiah was prophesying about Israel's future after her captivity to Babylon. She would once again thrive and grow, as a formerly barren woman who now begins to have many children.

"28 Now we, brethren, as Isaac was, are the children of promise.29 But as then he that was born after the flesh persecuted him that was born after the Spirit, even so it is now.30 Nevertheless what saith the scripture? Cast out the bondwoman and her son: for the son of the bondwoman shall not be heir with the son of the freewoman.31 So then, brethren, we are not children of the bondwoman, but of the free." Galatians 4:28-31.

At creation the Law of Selflessness was written in the hearts and minds of men, and they were naturally selfless. After the fall this principle of selflessness began to fade and self-serving became human nature.

After thousands of years the principle of selflessness was almost completely erased and so God saw it necessary to write a summation of the great Law of Selflessness in the form of the 10 Commandments which men could read and apply within their hearts. When they sinned, they could bring an animal sacrifice to obtain provisional forgiveness.

146

Both the application of the law to the heart and the bringing of an animal sacrifice was of works. This was the "Old Covenant," - salvation by works, which is depicted by Abraham's early experience when he took Hagar and they conceived, Ishmael.

In the New Covenant, the Law of Selflessness is written in the heart by the Holy Spirit as it was in Eden and selflessness again becomes the natural impulse of life. This transformation is granted to those who believe in the Holy Spirits power to transform the heart. When there is sin, faith in Christ's sacrifice cancels the sin, there is no need to apply the law to the heart nor bring an animal sacrifice. This is represented by the analogy of the latter experience of Abraham when he had faith in the promise of God that his barren wife would conceive a great nation.

Since there was nothing, he could do medically to make his barren wife Sarah conceive he simply had to trust God. Thus, we believe in God's power to justify us (wash away sin) and sanctify (change the heart to reflect selflessness) by faith, without any human devising.

"[7] And I will establish my covenant between me and thee and thy seed after thee in their generations for an everlasting covenant, to be a God unto thee, and to thy seed after thee. [8] And I will give unto thee, and to thy seed after thee, the land wherein thou art a stranger, all the land of Canaan, for an everlasting possession; and I will be their God." Genesis 17:7, 8.

The covenant made in Eden and renewed with Abraham consisted of two parts, a physical and spiritual part. The physical component included countless descendants and the physical land of Canaan. The second part, the spiritual component, included the Messiah who would redeem his people to inherit the heavenly Canaan. Both portions of the promise were dependent on faith and a reflection of the divine character of selflessness.

While Abraham was an inheritor of the literal land of Canaan, he did not count it as his true home, but he was a stranger and pilgrim heading toward the heavenly Canaan. Thus, Abraham was not only a sharer of the physical portions of the covenant, but he was also to share in the spiritual portions of the covenant. The land of Canaan was not the grand prize but a means to an end. It was a "stop over" until the promised heavenly Canaan would be realized. The purpose of the land of Canaan was to be a place where the descendants of Abraham could live separate from idolatry. Israel was to gradually enlarge her borders until the entire earth would be covered with the knowledge of the selfless character of God.

"**¹³ These all died in faith, not having received the promises, but having seen them afar off, and were persuaded of them, and embraced them, and confessed that they were strangers and pilgrims on the earth. ¹⁴ For they that say such things declare plainly that they seek a country. ¹⁵ And truly, if they had been mindful of that country from whence they came out, they might have had opportunity to have returned. ¹⁶ But now they desire a better country, that is, an heavenly: wherefore God is not ashamed to be called their God: for he hath prepared for them a city." Hebrews 11:13-16.**

"**²² But ye are come unto mount Sion, and unto the city of the living God, the heavenly Jerusalem, and to an innumerable company of angels," Hebrew 12:22. "¹⁴ For** here have we no continuing city, but we seek one to come." Hebrews 13:14.

ANALOGY OF THE TWO COVENANTS	
OLD COVENANT	**NEW COVENANT**
Covenant was made on Mt. Sinai	Covenant made in Eden
Ratified at Sinai in Arabia	Ratified at the cross in Jerusalem
Law written in stone	Law written in the heart
Certified with animals' blood	Certified with Christ's blood
Righteousness by works	Righteousness by faith
Read Law and apply to life	Law reflected from within
Human nature unchanged	Human nature changed
Covenant represented by Hagar- Ishmael	Covenant represented by Sarah- Isaac
Bond woman - human intervention	Free woman – divine intervention

CHAPTER 21
CIRCUMCISION A SIGN OF THE COVENANT

"¹⁰ This is my covenant, which ye shall keep, between me and you and thy seed after thee; Every man child among you shall be circumcised. ¹¹ And ye shall circumcise the flesh of your foreskin; and it shall be a token of the covenant betwixt me and you. ¹² And he that is eight days old shall be circumcised among you, every man child in your generations, he that is born in the house, or bought with money of any stranger, which is not of thy seed. ¹⁴ And the uncircumcised man child whose flesh of his foreskin is not circumcised, that soul shall be cut off from his people; he hath broken my covenant." Genesis 17:10-14.

The Covenant made in Eden and repeated to Abraham was to be celebrated by the ritual of circumcision. The sign of the covenant through all the generations was to be on the very organ of generation and was to be performed by every father as a promise and commitment to raise their sons within the covenant. The seed to be propagated was not to be merely any seed but a selfless seed.

The Jews in Paul's day had come to view circumcision as a merit by which they would be saved. Paul re-iterates as with the sabbath and festive observance that no amount of ritual would save a person, only the belief in Christ's power to forgive sins and change the character. But then to what purpose is ritual, whether it be circumcision, baptism, sabbath or festive observance? The purpose is the facilitation of sanctification.

These rituals bring memory and rehearsal of the great themes of salvation into the family unit. Children learn these great themes by practice, by repetition, by ritual. A first-born son watching his young brother being circumcised will naturally ask his father why this is so, thus presenting the father with an opportunity to explain the Covenant made in Eden, repeated to Abraham, and certified at the cross. When the first-born child now sees his own circumcision, he will be reminded of his high calling – this is the purpose of ritual. An orchestra for example can only perfect a symphony by the ritual of practice, practice does not win the prize, but the perfect notes produced at the final contest. Ritual does not save a man, it's a tool in the hand of the Holy Spirit to facilitate that salvation.

Circumcision was to be completed on the 8th day not at birth. In Biblical numerology the number 7 indicated perfection and the completion of a cycle as in the creative week. The number 8 in numerology indicates the start of a new cycle, a new beginning.

"⁶ And the LORD thy God will circumcise thine heart, and the heart of thy seed, to love the LORD thy God with all thine heart, and with all thy soul, that thou mayest live." Deuteronomy 30:6" ¹⁶ Circumcise therefore the foreskin of your heart, and be no more stiffnecked." Deuteronomy 10:6

The male foreskin is a natural barrier, and in these scriptures the foreskin of the heart represents the barrier between man and God and that barrier is self-serving. God will remove the foreskin of the heart, he will remove our self-serving natures which stands in the way, between man and God, a barrier to eternal life. Circumcision of the flesh was designed to be reflective of the circumcision of the heart. A child is circumcised on the 8th day without any understanding of its significance, but later they can choose to make their own commitment to the life of self-serving by the washing away of their sins by the ritual of baptism.

"25 For circumcision verily profiteth, if thou keep the law: but if thou be a breaker of the law, thy circumcision is made uncircumcision." Romans 2:25

Circumcision of the male organ was designed to be reflective of the work of the Holy Spirit on the heart. Paul states here that circumcision is only of benefit when the heart is reflective of the Law of Selflessness. If the heart is full of selfishness, it effectively negates or undoes the circumcision of the male organ.

"26 Therefore if the uncircumcision keep the righteousness of the law, shall not his uncircumcision be counted for circumcision?" Romans 2:26.

The "uncircumcision" in the first part of this text refers to the gentile converts who were uncircumcised. Paul here is asking the question for arguments sake: If the gentiles are reflective of the great Law of selflessness, will they not be accepted of God as though they were circumcised? Paul makes this argument because the Jews were self-righteous, they believed the mere act of circumcision would entitle them to heaven without the necessary work of the heart of which circumcision was only symbolic.

"27 And shall not uncircumcision which is by nature, if it fulfil the law, judge thee, who by the letter and circumcision dost transgress the law?" Romans 2:27.

Those uncircumcised gentile converts who were by nature selfless in heart were more acceptable to God than the caviling Jews who were circumcised in the flesh, by the letter, but not of the heart. Paul does not suggest that ritual is to be disregarded or dispensed with, but he was placing the importance of ritual in its correct light. Ritual does not save us, ritual is symbolic of a greater work, it only facilitates the sanctification process through repetition, education, and the creation of a national identity as the people of God.

"28 For he is not a Jew, which is one outwardly; neither is that circumcision, which is outward in the flesh: 29 But he is a Jew, which is one inwardly; and circumcision is that of the heart, in the spirit, and not in the letter; whose praise is not of men, but of God." Romans 2:28, 29.

Verses 28 and 29 are the main thrust of Paul's argument. A real Jew is not one who has merely had a circumcision of the male organ but one whose heart has been circumcised. A circumcised heart is one that has come under the transforming power of the Holy Spirit and has been changed from self-serving to selflessness. While men may see the circumcision of the male organ, in the flesh, it is God alone who sees the circumcision of the heart.

CHAPTER 22
ABRAHAM CALLED TO SACRIFICE ISAAC

"[1] And it came to pass after these things, that God did tempt Abraham, and said unto him, Abraham: and he said, Behold, here I am. [2] And he said, Take now thy son, thine only son Isaac, whom thou lovest, and get thee into the land of Moriah; and offer him there for a burnt offering upon one of the mountains which I will tell thee of." Genesis 22:1, 2.

Abraham had been called to be the father of a nation of trusting selfless people, but his faith had not yet been made fully perfect. He had shown a dependence on self when he suggested to adopt Eliezer, when he concealed Sarah's identity as his wife before the Egyptians and again when he took Hagar to be his wife.

This test to sacrifice his son was set that Abraham might fully experience and participate in the plan of redemption. This test was placed on record that his descendants might know what is expected of them as the seed of Abraham – a trusting heart in God's selfless decisions.

The Lord now directed Abraham to take his beloved son and heir of the promise through whom the Messiah would come and to offer Isaac as a sacrifice. Abraham was 100 years old when Isaac was born, and Isaac had since become a young man. This sacrifice was to be a willing sacrifice on the part of both father and son. The Bible says that God now "tempted" Abraham. "Tempted" is from the Hebrew word "nissah" which is rendered elsewhere in the King James

Version as "prove," since the scriptures declare that God tempts no man (James 1:13).

"**3 And Abraham rose up early in the morning, and saddled his ass, and took two of his young men with him, and Isaac his son, and clave the wood for the burnt offering, and rose up, and went unto the place of which God had told him." Genesis 22:3.**

Here we are given a brief account of his preparation, reflecting his faith. There was no trace of past moments of weakness. This was the climax of his spiritual experience, which qualified him for the high honor of being called "the father of the faithful."

"**4 Then on the third day Abraham lifted up his eyes, and saw the place afar off. 5 And Abraham said unto his young men, Abide ye here with the ass; and I and the lad will go yonder and worship, and come again to you." Genesis 22:4.**

After two days journey they arrived at Mt. Moriah. Abraham told his servants to wait at the base of the mountain for what he was to do was too sacred for human eyes to behold. Isaac was to be the first to know and he was the only one who was to share in the hour of his passion. In instructing the servants to wait for their return Abraham's faith is again demonstrated. Although Abraham could not understand the divine purpose in the sacrifice of his son the scriptures state that Abraham believed that "...God was able to raise him up, even from the dead." Hebrews 11:19. This was Abraham's belief, for God had promised that Isaac was to be the heir through whom the Messiah would come.

"⁶ And Abraham took the wood of the burnt offering, and laid it upon Isaac his son; and he took the fire in his hand, and a knife; and they went both of them together.⁷ And Isaac spake unto Abraham his father, and said, My father: and he said, Here am I, my son. And he said, Behold the fire and the wood: but where is the lamb for a burnt offering?⁸ And Abraham said, My son, God will provide himself a lamb for a burnt offering: so they went both of them together." Genesis 22:6-8.

Father and son made the hard ascent up the mountainside. Abraham assures Isaac that God Himself will provide the sacrificial victim. Reaching the summit of Moriah, Abraham now erected the altar. This site was of great significance and was designated by God himself. This very site where Abraham was to offer up his son in selflessness was to be the future site of Solomon's temple in Jerusalem and a little to the north was the site of Christ's selfless sacrifice at Calvary, all within view of the aged patriarch. But little did Abraham realize the significance of the act in offering his son at this location nor did he comprehend the significance of the sacrifice itself at that time.

"⁹ And they came to the place which God had told him of; and Abraham built an altar there, and laid the wood in order, and bound Isaac his son, and laid him on the altar upon the wood." Genesis 22:9.

Abraham had sacrificed many an animal, cutting its throat and laying it on an altar, but now to do this to his own precious son...? Isaac could have easily resisted his old father but from an early age he had been instructed in the lessons of faith and selflessness and he willingly surrendered himself. The fact that Isaac shared in his father's faith is a testament to the selfless parenting he received. Isaac now becomes a fitting representation of Christ who submitted to the will of His Father.

The last words of affection spoken, Abraham lifts the knife to his sons throat when the precious Savior Himself the "[11]...angel of the LORD called unto him out of heaven, and said, Abraham, Abraham: and he said, Here am I. [12] And he said, Lay not thine hand upon the lad, neither do thou any thing unto him: for now I know that thou fearest God, seeing thou hast not withheld thy son, thine only son from me." Genesis 22:11,12.

" [13] And Abraham lifted up his eyes, and looked, and behold behind him a ram caught in a thicket by his horns: and Abraham went and took the ram, and offered him up for a burnt offering in the stead of his son.[14] And Abraham called the name of that place Jehovahjireh: as it is said to this day, In the mount of the LORD it shall be seen." Genesis 22:12-14.

"[15] And the angel of the LORD called unto Abraham out of heaven the second time,[16] And said, By myself have I sworn, saith the LORD, for because thou hast done this thing, and hast not withheld thy son, thine only son:[17] That in blessing I will bless thee, and in multiplying I will multiply thy seed as the stars of the heaven, and as the sand which is upon the sea shore; and thy seed shall possess the gate of his enemies;[18] And in thy seed shall all the nations of the earth be blessed; because thou hast obeyed my voice.[19] So Abraham returned unto his young men, and they rose up and went together to Beersheba; and Abraham dwelt at Beersheba." Genesis 22:15-19.

God "preached before the gospel unto Abraham." Galatians 3:8. Through this experience Abraham was able to comprehend more clearly the plan of salvation. As a father himself he was able to understand more of the sacrifice that God the Father would make in giving up His Son to die for sinful man. In substituting the life of Isaac with the ram, Abraham saw himself the sinner whose life was required by law, substituted by the Lamb of God.

But with Christ there was no voice telling Him that His path to Calvary had demonstrated his faith and obedience and that His sacrifice was no longer required. God the Father gave Himself fully in the death of his Son. What Abraham experienced in part; God had experienced in full. Through this experience Abraham was able to comprehend more fully the great love of God in sending his son to die for man. For this reason, the Savior could say. "Your father Abraham rejoiced to see my day: and he saw it, and was glad." John 8:56.

CHAPTER 23

SODOM AND GOMORRAH

"**16 And the men rose up from thence, and looked toward Sodom: and Abraham went with them to bring them on the way. 17 And the LORD said, Shall I hide from Abraham that thing which I do; 18 Seeing that Abraham shall surely become a great and mighty nation, and all the nations of the earth shall be blessed in him? 19 For I know him, that he will command his children and his household after him, and they shall keep the way of the LORD, to do justice and judgment; that the LORD may bring upon Abraham that which he hath spoken of him."** Genesis 18:16-18.

The three angel travelers who dined at Abraham's table in Genesis 18 and who bore the news of Sarah's imminent conception are the same ones who now go down into Sodom and rescue Lot. According to the custom of friendship Abraham accompanied his guests upon their way for a short distance, when the Lord turns to the other two angels and says that He will reveal to Abraham the object of their mission. The Lord gives reason for this decision by referencing the covenant, and that Abraham will instruct his children using the destruction of Sodom as an important lesson in separation from the world.

"**20 And the LORD said, Because the cry of Sodom and Gomorrah is great, and because their sin is very grievous; 21 I will go down now, and see whether they have done altogether according to the cry of it, which is come unto me; and if not, I will know.22 And the men turned their faces from thence, and went toward Sodom:**

but Abraham stood yet before the LORD." Genesis 18:20-22.

Sodom and Gomorrah had reached the limit of the divine patience; their cup of self-serving was now full. The two angels departed to Sodom while the Lord remains behind with Abraham. Abraham now pleads with the Lord requesting that the righteous not be destroyed with the wicked.

"[23] And Abraham drew near, and said, Wilt thou also destroy the righteous with the wicked? [24] Peradventure there be fifty righteous within the city: wilt thou also destroy and not spare the place for the fifty righteous that are therein? [25] That be far from thee to do after this manner, to slay the righteous with the wicked: and that the righteous should be as the wicked, that be far from thee: Shall not the Judge of all the earth do right?

[26] And the LORD said, If I find in Sodom fifty righteous within the city, then I will spare all the place for their sakes. [27] And Abraham answered and said, Behold now, I have taken upon me to speak unto the Lord, which am but dust and ashes:" Genesis 18:23-27.

Abraham addresses the Lord as the "Judge" indicating that he clearly understood that the one he was speaking to was God. In humility Abraham requests mercy for the righteous inhabitants of the doomed city. The Lord had stated that the city would be spared if fifty righteous people could be found. Abraham decreases his count gradually down to 10, but even 10 could not be found (Genesis 18:32,33).

Abraham here displays the spirit of selfless intercession. Those who are self-righteous are very critical of others, they are faultfinders, but those who are justified by faith have a sense of their own unworthiness and dependence on divine mercy for salvation. "They got what they deserved" are words spoken by a heart that is self-righteous for if we got what "we deserved" then a crucifixion is all we would merit. Abraham had no secret joy in the destruction of the city.

"¹ And there came two angels to Sodom at even; and Lot sat in the gate of Sodom: and Lot seeing them rose up to meet them; and he bowed himself with his face toward the ground; ² And he said, Behold now, my lords, turn in, I pray you, into your servant's house, and tarry all night, and wash your feet, and ye shall rise up early, and go on your ways. And they said, Nay; but we will abide in the street all night.³ And he pressed upon them greatly; and they turned in unto him, and entered into his house; and he made them a feast, and did bake unleavened bread, and they did eat." Genesis 19:1-3.

The two angels that left Abraham and the Lord now arrive in Sodom. The distance from Abraham's home in Hebron to Sodom was about 25 miles. The first to greet them at the gate was Lot. Years before Lot had pitched his tent on the outskirts of Sodom (Genesis 13:12) but since that time he had built a house within the city. Lot met the apparent strangers at the city gate and invited them to his home but they initially declined but accepted following his persistence.

"⁴ But before they lay down, the men of the city, even the men of Sodom, compassed the house round, both old and young, all the people from every quarter: ⁵ And they

called unto Lot, and said unto him, Where are the men which came in to thee this night? bring them out unto us, that we may know them." Genesis 19:4, 5.

The news of the strangers was soon made known and the men of Sodom, both young and old, with homosexual desires gathered around Lot's home demanding the strangers be released to them. Their purpose was to "know them," sexually. "[27] And likewise also the men, leaving the natural use of the woman, burned in their lust one toward another; men with men working that which is unseemly, and receiving in themselves that recompense of their error which was meet." Romans 1:24-27. "[13] If a man also lie with mankind, as he lieth with a woman, both of them have committed an abomination: they shall surely be put to death; their blood shall be upon them." Leviticus 20:13.

Sadly, many men who engage in this lifestyle have often been initiated into it by early childhood sexual trauma and many times have no recollection of the event ever occurring. For those who choose freedom from this curse, God is ready to forgive and to heal and will welcome them with loving arms. The men of Sodom however were non-repentant.

"[6] And Lot went out at the door unto them, and shut the door after him,[7] And said, I pray you, brethren, do not so wickedly.[8] Behold now, I have two daughters which have not known man; let me, I pray you, bring them out unto you, and do ye to them as is good in your eyes: only unto these men do nothing; for therefore came they under the shadow of my roof.[9] And they said, Stand back. And they said again, This one fellow came in to sojourn, and he will needs be a judge: now will we deal worse with thee, than with them. And they pressed sore upon the man, even Lot, and came near to break the door." Genesis 19:6-9.

It is an oriental custom to defend one's guests unto death. Accordingly, Lot now proposes to bring his daughters out to them instead of turning his guests over to be molested. The Bible states Lot was "a just man" (2 Peter 2:7) and his offer to bring out his daughters was to shame them of their homosexual desires. The crowd became indignant that Lot, a nonnative of Sodom, should be homophobic and dare pass judgment on them.

"¹⁰ But the men put forth their hand, and pulled Lot into the house to them, and shut to the door.¹¹ And they smote the men that were at the door of the house with blindness, both small and great: so that they wearied themselves to find the door.

¹² And the men said unto Lot, Hast thou here any besides? son in law, and thy sons, and thy daughters, and whatsoever thou hast in the city, bring them out of this place:¹³ For we will destroy this place, because the cry of them is waxen great before the face of the LORD; and the LORD hath sent us to destroy it." Genesis 19:10-13.

The angels pulled Lot into the house and struck the mob with confusion thus preventing them from locating the door to the house. They informed Lot of their intent to destroy the city, urging him and all his family to prepare for immediate departure.

"¹⁴ And Lot went out, and spake unto his sons in law, which married his daughters, and said, Up, get you out of this place; for the LORD will destroy this city. But he seemed as one that mocked unto his sons in law." Genesis 19: 14.

Lot had stated earlier that he had two virgin daughters and now it is stated that he spoke to his "sons in law" indicating that Lot had at least four daughters since sons in law is spoken of as plural. Lot had told his family that the city was to be destroyed but they dismissed him as a fanatic.

"[15] And when the morning arose, then the angels hastened Lot, saying, Arise, take thy wife, and thy two daughters, which are here; lest thou be consumed in the iniquity of the city.[16] And while he lingered, the men laid hold upon his hand, and upon the hand of his wife, and upon the hand of his two daughters; the LORD being merciful unto him: and they brought him forth, and set him without the city." Genesis 19:15, 16.

At daybreak the angels instruct Lot to escape the doomed city. Lot and his wife believed but found it difficult to leave their home and their possessions that had taken a lifetime to accumulate. The two angels who showed no concern for their possessions grabbed the hands of Lot, his wife and his two daughters and rushed them out of the city. Such is the marvel that even a just man can become so infatuated with the things of this world that he finds it difficult to tear himself free from it even in the face of certain death.

"[17] And it came to pass, when they had brought them forth abroad, that he said, Escape for thy life; look not behind thee, neither stay thou in all the plain; escape to the mountain, lest thou be consumed. [18] And Lot said unto them, Oh, not so, my Lord: [19] Behold now, thy servant hath found grace in thy sight, and thou hast magnified thy mercy, which thou hast shewed unto me in saving my life; and I cannot escape to the mountain, lest some evil take me, and I die: ²⁰ Behold now, this city is near to flee unto, and it is a little one: Oh, let me escape thither, (is it not a little one?) and my soul shall live.

²¹ And he said unto him, See, I have accepted thee concerning this thing also, that I will not overthrow this city, for the which thou hast spoken.²² Haste thee, escape thither; for I cannot do any thing till thou be come thither. Therefore the name of the city was called Zoar.²³ The sun was risen upon the earth when Lot entered into Zoar.

²⁴ Then the LORD rained upon Sodom and upon Gomorrah brimstone and fire from the LORD out of heaven; ²⁵ And he overthrew those cities, and all the plain, and all the inhabitants of the cities, and that which grew upon the ground.²⁶ But his wife looked back from behind him, and she became a pillar of salt." Genesis 19:17-26.

The Lord who had remained behind with Abraham while the two angels went down into Sodom now joins the company. How tragic had been Lot's decision to leave the countryside alongside Abraham for city living in Sodom. Self now pleads with the Lord that he might be permitted to go to another city called Zoar. Lot was reluctant to leave the ease and luxury of city life for what appeared to him a difficult and uncertain lifestyle amongst the mountains.

Lot was determined that he knew better, and the Lord permitted his request that he might see yet once more the results of trusting in self. Today the southern portions of the Dead Sea with its dry landscape remain a testimony to the catastrophe that turned the fertile valley, once compared to the "garden of the Lord," to a scene of utter desolation.

Lot's wife lingering on the plain was overcome by the noxious fumes of sulfur and turned into a mound of organic salt by the intense heat. While her body was on the plain her heart still clung to Sodom where her family and her possessions lay. This experience of Lot's wife is a testimony to all who would like to be saved but are not willing to die to self and defer all to God's perfect judgment. They seem to forsake the world, but their hearts are still in it.

"**27 And Abraham gat up early in the morning to the place where he stood before the LORD:28 And he looked toward Sodom and Gomorrah, and toward all the land of the plain, and beheld, and, lo, the smoke of the country went up as the smoke of a furnace.29 And it came to pass, when God destroyed the cities of the plain, that God remembered Abraham, and sent Lot out of the midst of the overthrow, when he overthrew the cities in the which Lot dwelt." Genesis 19:27-29.**

Abraham arose the following morning and travelled to the location overlooking the plain where he and the Lord had spoken only to behold a scene of utter destruction.

The Descendants of Lot

"30 And Lot went up out of Zoar, and dwelt in the mountain, and his two daughters with him; for he feared to dwell in Zoar: and he dwelt in a cave, he and his two daughters.31 And the firstborn said unto the younger, Our father is old, and there is not a man in the earth to come in unto us after the manner of all the earth: 32 Come, let us make our father drink wine, and we will lie

with him, that we may preserve seed of our father.[33] And they made their father drink wine that night: and the firstborn went in, and lay with her father; and he perceived not when she lay down, nor when she arose.

[34] And it came to pass on the morrow, that the firstborn said unto the younger, Behold, I lay yesternight with my father: let us make him drink wine this night also; and go thou in, and lie with him, that we may preserve seed of our father.[35] And they made their father drink wine that night also: and the younger arose, and lay with him; and he perceived not when she lay down, nor when she arose.

[36] Thus were both the daughters of Lot with child by their father.[37] And the firstborn bare a son, and called his name Moab: the same is the father of the Moabites unto this day.[38] And the younger, she also bare a son, and called his name Benammi: the same is the father of the children of Ammon unto this day." Genesis 19:30-38

Lot, terrified that Zoar would be destroyed, abandoned the city, and made his home in a cave. His daughters, having brought their father to intoxication through wine now deliberately conceived bearing children. Living in the self-serving city the lines of morality were blurred. The Moabites and the Ammonites, the result of the union between Lot and his daughters, were idolatrous tribes that were a continual threat to Israel.

Lot together with Abraham left Babylonia with a willing heart but he soon became tired of country living. Instead of "passing through" as a Hebrew he desired to be a resident of this world, he separated from Abraham amongst the hills and made his home in the city, a place proverbial for its wickedness. The destruction of Lot's nuclear family unit is a reminder for all times as to the evils of associating with those in the service of self.

"**26** **And as it was in the days of Noe, so shall it be also in the days of the Son of man.**[27] **They did eat, they drank, they married wives, they were given in marriage, until the day that Noe entered into the ark, and the flood came, and destroyed them all.**[28] **Likewise also as it was in the days of Lot; they did eat, they drank, they bought, they sold, they planted, they builded;**

[29] **But the same day that Lot went out of Sodom it rained fire and brimstone from heaven, and destroyed them all.**[30] **Even thus shall it be in the day when the Son of man is revealed.**[31] **In that day, he which shall be upon the housetop, and his stuff in the house, let him not come down to take it away: and he that is in the field, let him likewise not return back.**[32] **Remember Lot's wife." Luke 17:26-32.**

The story of Sodom and Gomorrah is about the fragmentation of Lot's nuclear family unit caused by raising his children in metaphorical "Babylon." Lots daughters received of its self-serving mold which they transmitted to their descendants who were forever the enemies of God and His people.

How different would have been their life's history had they remained with Abraham in the countryside participating in the covenant of salvation, the very purpose for which they were called out of Ur in greater Babylon. Today mothers are called to "remember Lot's wife" and her critical error in choosing to raise her children in the cities of this world, the place where self-serving has been perfected to a science.

SECTION V
JACOB AND ESAU

CHAPTER 24

THE BIRTH OF JACOB AND ESAU

The Marriage of Isaac and Rebekah

"¹ And Sarah was an hundred and seven and twenty years old: these were the years of the life of Sarah. ² And Sarah died in Kirjatharba; the same is Hebron in the land of Canaan: and Abraham came to mourn for Sarah, and to weep for her..." Genesis 23:1, 2.

After a long and eventful life Sarah died at the age of 127. She was 90 when Isaac was born thus Isaac was 37 years old at her death (Genesis 17:1,17; 21:5). Abraham laid Sarah to rest in Mamre, their home before Isaac was born. Here they shared their sorrows and joys all within a short distance from her grave.

"² And Abraham said unto his eldest servant of his house, that ruled over all that he had, Put, I pray thee, ..that thou shalt not take a wife unto my son of the daughters of the Canaanites, among whom I dwell:⁴ But thou shalt go unto my country, and to my kindred, and take a wife unto my son Isaac...⁶ And Abraham said unto him, Beware thou that thou bring not my son thither again. ⁷ The LORD God of heaven, which took me from my father's house, and from the land of my kindred." Genesis 24:2, 4, 6, 7.

Three years following the death of Sarah, Abraham sent his servant back to Haran in upper Mesopotamia to his brother Nahor to find a wife for his now 40-year-old son Isaac. Abraham knew his brother's house had some knowledge of the true God and a wife from there would be preferable to a godless Canaanite. Abraham did not want

Isaac to be corrupted by a visit to Haran and so he sent his servant. Isaac trusted God's choice in this arranged marriage knowing that God sees all and knows all. The wife who would be chosen would have to be willing to leave her family behind to become an inheritor of the promise.

"[10] **And the servant took ten camels of the camels of his master, and departed; for all the goods of his master were in his hand: and he arose, and went to Mesopotamia, unto the city of Nahor.[11] And he made his camels to kneel down without the city by a well of water at the time of the evening, even the time that women go out to draw water.**

[12] **And he said, O LORD God of my master Abraham, I pray thee, send me good speed this day, and shew kindness unto my master Abraham.** [13] **Behold, I stand here by the well of water; and the daughters of the men of the city come out to draw water:** [14] **And let it come to pass, that the damsel to whom I shall say, Let down thy pitcher, I pray thee, that I may drink;**

…[15] **And it came to pass, before he had done speaking, that, behold, Rebekah came out, who was born to Bethuel, son of Milcah, the wife of Nahor, Abraham's brother, with her pitcher upon her shoulder." Genesis 24: 10-15**

"[16] **And the damsel was very fair to look upon, a virgin, neither had any man known her: and she went down to the well, and filled her pitcher, and came up.** [17] **And the servant ran to meet her, and said, Let me, I pray thee, drink a little water of thy pitcher.** [18] **And she said, Drink, my lord: and she hasted, and let down her pitcher**

172

upon her hand, and gave him drink...

 ²³ And said, Whose daughter art thou? tell me, I pray thee: is there room in thy father's house for us to lodge in?²⁴ And she said unto him, I am the daughter of Bethuel the son of Milcah, which she bare unto Nahor. ²⁵ She said moreover unto him, We have both straw and provender enough, and room to lodge in.²⁶ And the man bowed down his head, and worshipped the LORD..."

⁵⁰ Then Laban and Bethuel answered and said, The thing proceedeth from the LORD: we cannot speak unto thee bad or good. ⁵¹ Behold, Rebekah is before thee, take her, and go, and let her be thy master's son's wife, as the LORD hath spoken... ⁵⁸ And they called Rebekah, and said unto her, Wilt thou go with this man? And she said, I will go. ...⁶¹ And Rebekah arose, and her damsels, and they rode upon the camels, and followed the man: and the servant took Rebekah, and went his way." Genesis 24:10-18, 23-26, 50, 51, 58, 61.

Abraham's servant, Rebekah and her handmaiden now made the long journey back to Canaan to marry a man she had never met. If this was the will of the Lord then no other man could make her happy, for they had been chosen for each other by divine appointment.

The Birth of Jacob and Esau

"¹⁹ And these are the generations of Isaac, Abraham's son: Abraham begat Isaac: ²⁰ And Isaac was forty years old when he took Rebekah to wife, the daughter of Bethuel the Syrian of Padanaram, the sister to Laban the Syrian.²¹ And Isaac intreated the LORD for his wife, because she was barren: and the LORD was intreated of

him, and Rebekah his wife conceived." Genesis 25:19-21.

Isaac was 40 years old when he married Rebekah, but after 19 years of a childless marriage Isaac and Rebekah prayed and the Lord blessed them with twin boys.

"[22] And the children struggled together within her; and she said, If it be so, why am I thus? And she went to enquire of the LORD. [23] And the LORD said unto her, Two nations are in thy womb, and two manner of people shall be separated from thy bowels; and the one people shall be stronger than the other people; and the elder shall serve the younger. [24] And when her days to be delivered were fulfilled, behold, there were twins in her womb." Genesis 25:22-24.

Mankind still had a relatively open connection with heaven and Rebekah prayed to the Lord regarding the mysterious movements in her womb and the Lord revealed to her the future of her two sons. The struggle that she felt between them was the spirit of enmity foretold in Eden that would exist between the selfless and the self-serving. The antagonism between the "seed of the women," the descendants of Jacob, and the seed of the serpent, the descendants of Esau, the Edomites, would play out in history. The Edomites were ever the enemies of Israel.

"[25] And the first came out red, all over like an hairy garment; and they called his name Esau. [26] And after that came his brother out, and his hand took hold on Esau's heel; and his name was called Jacob: and Isaac was threescore years old when she bare them." Genesis 25:25, 26.

Esau and Jacob were fraternal twins. Esau came out first followed immediately by Jacob who came on the heel of his brother therefore they called him Jacob, from the Hebrew word "aqeb" meaning "heel catcher," figuratively meaning to "deceive." Isaac was now 60 years old; Grandfather Abraham was therefore 160 years old (Genesis 21:5). The twins were 15 when Abraham died at the age of 175. (Genesis 25:8).

The Fracturing of the Nuclear Family Unit

"27 And the boys grew: and Esau was a cunning hunter, a man of the field; and Jacob was a plain man, dwelling in tents." Genesis 25:27.

As the boys grew, a marked difference was seen in their physical appearance and characters. Esau was a "cunning hunter," he was a strong, athletic hairy man leading a wild adventurous life. Jacob was smooth skinned and was said to be "plain," indicating he was more cultured and refined, enjoying the responsibilities of settled family life.

"28 And Isaac loved Esau, because he did eat of his venison: but Rebekah loved Jacob." Genesis 25:28.

This once promising family unit was now fractured by the self-serving trait of favoritism. Isaac naturally gravitated toward Esau's adventurous life and Rebekah identified more with the calm peaceful spirit of Jacob. While this gravitational pull is a natural phenomenon, an issue occurs when this leads to a different set of rules and different standards of accountability applied to the different children. As children are growing, parents are to give fair and consistent rules with fair and consistent accountability for all their children, thus maintaining a cohesive nuclear family unit.

Isaac and Rebekah evidently "were not on the same page" when it came to disciplining their children. They could not agree on a parenting strategy behind closed doors because of favoritism to their children. Isaac likely felt Rebekah was too stern with Esau and Rebekah likely felt Isaac was too loose with Esau. This allows two children to play their parents against each other to achieve their self-serving agendas, invariably splitting the parents further and further apart.

Parents instead of confiding in one another in raising their children now learn to confide in their favorite child, changing the relationship to a permissive friendship. Rules are broken but accountability is lacking based on the new friendship dynamic. The parent in this new relationship is afraid to hold their child accountable in fear of rejection or facing their wrath thus allowing them "to get away with murder," and in this case with cruel deception.

Had Isaac and Rebekah been united in selflessness, then following the will of God to transfer the birthright to Jacob would never have been a question. But Isaac was allied with Esau and was not willing to disappoint him or face his wrath. Confirmation of the birthright would incite rebellion of Rebekah who was allied with Jacob, so he intended to confer the birthright in secret "to keep the peace."

Rebekah, who was allied with Jacob and not wanting to disappoint him, now approved of a plan to deceive her husband and have the birthright conferred on her favorite son. The result of this "favorite" dynamic led to the fracture of the nuclear family unit with subsequent development of serious character defects in either child, playing out for generations to come. The effects of favoritism are recorded in the word of God as a caution to subsequent generations seeking to raise children to reflect the divine image of selflessness.

CHAPTER 25

JACOB DECEIVES HIS FATHER

"²⁹ And Jacob sod pottage: and Esau came from the field, and he was faint:³⁰ And Esau said to Jacob, Feed me, I pray thee, with that same red pottage; for I am faint: therefore was his name called Edom.³¹ And Jacob said, Sell me this day thy birthright.³² And Esau said, Behold, I am at the point to die: and what profit shall this birthright do to me? ³³ And Jacob said, Swear to me this day; and he sware unto him: and he sold his birthright unto Jacob.³⁴ Then Jacob gave Esau bread and pottage of lentiles; and he did eat and drink, and rose up, and went his way: thus Esau despised his birthright." Genesis 25: 29-34.

Favoritism had fostered competition between the two brothers, seeking their own interests ahead of the other. A selfless heart would have furnished his brother with a warm bowl of lentils. Jacob had become an opportunist in this competitive relationship for supremacy, offering him food in exchange for the birthright.

The birthright entitled a person to three promises: a double portion of their father's estate, the position as the priest of the house and the honor of being the progenitor of the promised Messiah. The blessings of the birthright were intended for the firstborn on condition of character but when character was lacking the birthright was transferred to the one who was seeking to reflect the divine image.

Esau disregarded the requirements of the covenant to remain separate from idolaters by taking himself godless wives of Canaan (Genesis 26:34,35). It would be impossible for the Messiah to descend through a line of one who disregarded the provision of separation from the world.

The transfer from Esau to Jacob would have occurred in the Lord's time as God had indicated prior to their birth when Rebekah was told the older would serve the younger. Jacob, not willing to wait for the Lord's timing resorted to craft and purchased the birthright from Esau who cared not for the eternal inheritance given to him at birth.

"[1] And it came to pass, that when Isaac was old, and his eyes were dim, so that he could not see, he called Esau his eldest son, and said unto him, My son: and he said unto him, Behold, here am I.[2] And he said, Behold now, I am old, I know not the day of my death: [3] Now therefore take, I pray thee, thy weapons, thy quiver and thy bow, and go out to the field, and take me some venison; [4] And make me savoury meat, such as I love, and bring it to me, that I may eat; that my soul may bless thee..." Genesis 27:1-4.

Isaac was probably 137 years old and Jacob 77 when this incident occurred. With the infirmities of age creeping up Isaac must have evidently felt that his end was near, and he called his son to convey the birthright blessing. Isaac however lived another 43 years and died at the age of 180. He lived to witness the birth of Jacob's 12 sons.

"[5] And Rebekah heard when Isaac spake to Esau his son. And Esau went to the field to hunt for venison, and to bring it.[6] And Rebekah spake unto Jacob her son, saying, Behold, I heard thy father speak unto Esau thy brother, saying,[7] Bring me venison, and make me savoury meat, that I may eat, and bless thee before the LORD before my death.

[8] Now therefore, my son, obey my voice according to that which I command thee.[9] Go now to the flock, and fetch me from thence two good kids of the goats; and I will make them savoury meat for thy father, such as he loveth:[10] And thou shalt bring it to thy father, that he may eat, and that he may bless thee before his death.

[11] And Jacob said to Rebekah his mother, Behold, Esau my brother is a hairy man, and I am a smooth man: [12] My father peradventure will feel me, and I shall seem to him as a deceiver; and I shall bring a curse upon me, and not a blessing.[13] And his mother said unto him, Upon me be thy curse, my son: only obey my voice, and go fetch me them.[14] And he went, and fetched, and brought them to his mother: and his mother made savoury meat, such as his father loved.

[15] And Rebekah took goodly raiment of her eldest son Esau, which were with her in the house, and put them upon Jacob her younger son:[16] And she put the skins of the kids of the goats upon his hands, and upon the smooth of his neck:[17] And she gave the savoury meat and the bread, which she had prepared, into the hand of her son Jacob.

[18] And he came unto his father, and said, My father: and he said, Here am I; who art thou, my son?[19] And Jacob said unto his father, I am Esau thy firstborn; I have done according as thou badest me: arise, I pray thee, sit and eat of my venison, that thy soul may bless me.[20] And Isaac said unto his son, How is it that thou hast found it so quickly, my son? And he said, Because the LORD thy God brought it to me.

[21] And Isaac said unto Jacob, Come near, I pray thee, that I may feel thee, my son, whether thou be my very son Esau or not.[22] And Jacob went near unto Isaac his father; and he felt him, and said, The voice is Jacob's voice, but the hands are the hands of Esau.[23] And he discerned him not, because his hands were hairy, as his brother Esau's hands: so he blessed him.

[24] And he said, Art thou my very son Esau? And he said, I am. [25] And he said, Bring it near to me, and I will eat of my son's venison, that my soul may bless thee. And he brought it near to him, and he did eat: and he brought him wine, and he drank.

[26] And his father Isaac said unto him, Come near now, and kiss me, my son. [27] And he came near, and kissed him: and he smelled the smell of his raiment, and blessed him, and said, See, the smell of my son is as the smell of a field which the LORD hath blessed:" Genesis 27:5-27.

Entering his father's tent, Jacob was now confronted with several embarrassing questions. Convincing his father was no easy task. One deception after another was necessary to accomplish his design. He declared himself to be Esau, the kid's meat to be venison and his soon return due to the favor of the Lord. From Isaac's perspective the touch was like Esau, the smell was like Esau, but the voice was like Jacobs. These apparent inconsistencies of warning were forgotten, and caution was thrown to the wind.

"[28] Therefore God give thee of the dew of heaven, and the fatness of the earth, and plenty of corn and wine:[29] Let people serve thee, and nations bow down to thee: be lord over thy brethren, and let thy mother's sons bow down to thee: cursed be every one that curseth thee, and blessed be he that blesseth thee." Genesis 27:28, 29.

The aged patriarch now pronounced a blessing upon Jacob depicting him prosperous in the land of Canaan and the universal dominion of Israel which was God's original plan (Genesis 27:25-29). Although Jacob deceived Isaac, what he said was divinely inspired. God did not condone the act of deception, but He overruled it. Jacob scarcely departed from the tent when his brother Esau returned.

"[30] And it came to pass, as soon as Isaac had made an end of blessing Jacob, and Jacob was yet scarce gone out from the presence of Isaac his father, that Esau his brother came in from his hunting.[31] And he also had made savoury meat, and brought it unto his father, and said unto his father, Let my father arise, and eat of his son's venison, that thy soul may bless me.

[32] And Isaac his father said unto him, Who art thou? And he said, I am thy son, thy firstborn Esau.[33] And Isaac trembled very exceedingly, and said, Who? where is he that hath taken venison, and brought it me, and I have eaten of all before thou camest, and have blessed him? yea, and he shall be blessed.[34] And when Esau heard the words of his father, he cried with a great and exceeding bitter cry, and said unto his father, Bless me, even me also, O my father.[35] And he said, Thy brother came with subtilty, and hath taken away thy blessing.[36] And he said, Is not he rightly named Jacob? for he hath supplanted me these two times: he took away my birthright; and, behold, now he hath taken away my blessing. And he said, Hast thou not reserved a blessing for me?" Genesis 27:30-36.

Esau now cried that Jacob has lived up to his name as a deceiver. Esau did not realize that his defective character disqualified him from receiving the blessings of the covenant. He asked his father for a blessing as though Isaac had power to grant the blessing upon him. He did not understand that only by true repentance and turning away from sin could he receive the blessing. Esau coveted the blessing without any intention of accepting the obligations of developing a selfless character.

Esau cared nothing for the spiritual portion of the birthright. He cared not to be the priest of the family. He cared not for the privilege of being the progenitor of the promised Messiah. He cared only to be the inheritor of his father's estate. He desired the earthly blessings that came along with obedience. By taking wives from amongst the idolaters he clearly declared that he had no intention of the spiritual portion of the birthright. He did not desire the sanctified life that comes by faith.

Today men crave the blessing of eternal life but are not willing to follow the path of selflessness and in this they are "profane" men and women as was Esau. As Esau wept bitterly so shall they on that day of Final Accounts, "[28] There shall be weeping and gnashing of teeth, when ye shall see Abraham, and Isaac, and Jacob, and all the prophets, in the kingdom of God, and you yourselves thrust out." (Luke 13:28).

"[41] And Esau hated Jacob because of the blessing wherewith his father blessed him: and Esau said in his heart, The days of mourning for my father are at hand; then will I slay my brother Jacob. [42] And these words of Esau her elder son were told to Rebekah: and she sent and called Jacob her younger son, and said unto him,

183

Behold, thy brother Esau, as touching thee, doth comfort himself, purposing to kill thee.

"[43] Now therefore, my son, obey my voice; and arise, flee thou to Laban my brother to Haran; [44] And tarry with him a few days, until thy brother's fury turn away; [45] Until thy brother's anger turn away from thee, and he forget that which thou hast done to him: then I will send, and fetch thee from thence: why should I be deprived also of you both in one day? [46] And Rebekah said to Isaac, I am weary of my life because of the daughters of Heth: if Jacob take a wife of the daughters of Heth, such as these which are of the daughters of the land, what good shall my life do me?" Genesis 27:41-46.

Rebekah hearing that Esau was planning to kill his brother after the death of Isaac decided to send him to Haran to be with her brother Laban allowing Esau time to cool. If Esau should slay his brother, then the other members of the household according to law could execute judgment by taking the life of the murderer, thus she would lose two sons in one day. Rebekah then convinces Isaac of the plan for then Jacob may also find himself a wife amongst the professed worshipers of God. The thought of having an additional daughter-in-law who was an idolater would be intolerable.

"[1] And Isaac called Jacob, and blessed him, and charged him, and said unto him, Thou shalt not take a wife of the daughters of Canaan. [2] Arise, go to Padanaram, to the house of Bethuel thy mother's father; and take thee a wife from thence of the daughters of Laban thy mother's brother. [3] And God Almighty bless thee, and make thee fruitful, and multiply thee, that thou mayest be a multitude of people; [4] And give thee the

184

blessing of Abraham, to thee, and to thy seed with thee; that thou mayest inherit the land wherein thou art a stranger, which God gave unto Abraham.[5] And Isaac sent away Jacob: and he went to Padanaram unto Laban, son of Bethuel the Syrian, the brother of Rebekah, Jacob's and Esau's mother." Genesis 28:1-5.

Isaac had finally come to his senses, and he again repeated the covenant blessings instructing him to go to Haran that he might find a wife from amongst his mother's family. Jacob now left his home to make the long journey across the desert to a strange land to be amongst strangers. While Jacob departed, burdened with guilt, he was nevertheless now in possession of the birthright and of the blessings promised to Abraham.

CHAPTER 26

JACOB'S NEW LIFE IN EXILE

"[10] And Jacob went out from Beersheba, and went toward Haran.[11] And he lighted upon a certain place, and tarried there all night, because the sun was set; and he took of the stones of that place, and put them for his pillows, and lay down in that place to sleep.[12] And he dreamed, and behold a ladder set up on the earth, and the top of it reached to heaven: and behold the angels of God ascending and descending on it.

[13] And, behold, the LORD stood above it, and said, I am the LORD God of Abraham thy father, and the God of Isaac: the land whereon thou liest, to thee will I give it, and to thy seed;[14] And thy seed shall be as the dust of the earth, and thou shalt spread abroad to the west, and to the east, and to the north, and to the south: and in thee and in thy seed shall all the families of the earth be blessed.

[15] And, behold, I am with thee, and will keep thee in all places whither thou goest, and will bring thee again into this land; for I will not leave thee, until I have done that which I have spoken to thee of." Genesis 28:10-15.

Jacob was now an exile from his home and came to rest for the night at Luz. Luz was about 50 miles north of Beersheba, approximately 2 days journey from his home. In a dream the Lord revealed to Jacob exactly what he needed, a Savior. The ladder represented Jesus (John 1:51) who is the uninterrupted channel between the family in heaven and the family on earth. As the gospel had been preached to Abraham through the sacrifice of his son now the gospel is opened more clearly to Jacob that he might know that there is one mediator between God and man. Although he did not understand this to be Jesus, he understood that there was an unobstructed channel between himself and God.

"**¹⁶ And Jacob awaked out of his sleep, and he said, Surely the LORD is in this place; and I knew it not.¹⁷ And he was afraid, and said, How dreadful is this place! this is none other but the house of God, and this is the gate of heaven.¹⁸ And Jacob rose up early in the morning, and took the stone that he had put for his pillows, and set it up for a pillar, and poured oil upon the top of it.¹⁹ And he called the name of that place Bethel: but the name of that city was called Luz at the first." Genesis 28:16-19.**

Through this dream the covenant made in Eden, repeated to Abraham, was now conferred upon Jacob. Jacob could not purchase this birthright to be the progenitor of the Messiah by the sale of some food. But through this dream God conferred the birthright upon Jacob which would have occurred had Jacob waited on the Lord's timing.

This dream was the first step in Jacobs's long path of sanctification. It was here that his re-education was to begin. While he declared to be a worshipper of God, craving the spiritual blessings that entitled him to be a progenitor of the Messiah and the priest of the house, Jacob's heart and mind were full of self as evidenced by his shameful deception of his father. Jacob was to be "born again," his self-serving nature was to be replaced with a selfless nature, and here is where the new birth began.

"20 And Jacob vowed a vow, saying, If God will be with me, and will keep me in this way that I go, and will give me bread to eat, and raiment to put on, 21 So that I come again to my father's house in peace; then shall the LORD be my God: 22 And this stone, which I have set for a pillar, shall be God's house: and of all that thou shalt give me I will surely give the tenth unto thee." Genesis 28:20-22.

The stone was set up as a reminder of his repentance, of his new beginning in walking in the selfless ways of God. Jacob was not seeking to make terms with God, but these words were spoken in gratitude and humility after his shameful conduct in obtaining the birthright by fraud. Jacob's pledge to pay tithe was an acknowledgement of God's ownership overall, including himself, and that he would now walk in the path of selflessness.

"1Then Jacob went on his journey, and came into the land of the people of the east.2 And he looked, and behold a well in the field, and, lo, there were three flocks of sheep lying by it; ..." Genesis 29:1, 2.

After an approximate three-week journey of over 450 miles Jacob arrived in the vicinity of Haran, where he comes to meet his cousin Rachel at a well of water.

"10 And it came to pass, when Jacob saw Rachel the daughter of Laban his mother's brother, and the sheep of Laban his mother's brother, that Jacob went near, and rolled the stone from the well's mouth, and watered the flock of Laban his mother's brother.11 And Jacob kissed Rachel, and lifted up his voice, and wept.12 And Jacob told Rachel that he was her father's brother, and

that he was Rebekah's son: and she ran and told her father.[13] And it came to pass, when Laban heard the tidings of Jacob his sister's son, that he ran to meet him, and embraced him, and kissed him, and brought him to his house. And he told Laban all these things.[14] And Laban said to him, Surely thou art my bone and my flesh. And he abode with him the space of a month.

[15] And Laban said unto Jacob, Because thou art my brother, shouldest thou therefore serve me for nought? tell me, what shall thy wages be?[16] And Laban had two daughters: the name of the elder was Leah, and the name of the younger was Rachel. [17] Leah was tender eyed; but Rachel was beautiful and well favoured.[18] And Jacob loved Rachel; and said, I will serve thee seven years for Rachel thy younger daughter.[19] And Laban said, It is better that I give her to thee, than that I should give her to another man: abide with me.

[20] And Jacob served seven years for Rachel; and they seemed unto him but a few days, for the love he had to her.[21] And Jacob said unto Laban, Give me my wife, for my days are fulfilled, that I may go in unto her.[22] And Laban gathered together all the men of the place, and made a feast.

[23] And it came to pass in the evening, that he took Leah his daughter, and brought her to him; and he went in unto her.[24] And Laban gave unto his daughter Leah Zilpah his maid for an handmaid.[25] And it came to pass, that in the morning, behold, it was Leah: and he said to Laban, What is this thou hast done unto me? did not I serve with thee for Rachel? wherefore then hast thou beguiled me?" Genesis 29:10-25.

Jacob on arriving in Haran was united with his mother's family. Here he fell in love with Rachel and agreed to work for seven years for her hand in marriage. When it came time for their union, the crafty Laban substituted her sister Leah. In the east the custom was that the wedding would last one week, and the bride would be brought to the bridegroom veiled at night. The following morning Jacob the master deceiver woke up to find himself deceived for he found not Rachel at his side in the marital room but her sister.

"**[26] And Laban said, It must not be so done in our country, to give the younger before the firstborn. [27] Fulfil her week, and we will give thee this also for the service which thou shalt serve with me yet seven other years.[28] And Jacob did so, and fulfilled her week: and he gave him Rachel his daughter to wife also.[29] And Laban gave to Rachel his daughter Bilhah his handmaid to be her maid.[30] And he went in also unto Rachel, and he loved also Rachel more than Leah, and served with him yet seven other years." Genesis 29:26-30.**

Laban now appeals to a non-existent social custom that the eldest child was to be given away in wedlock before the youngest. Laban, now to save face in front of his guests, agreed with Jacob to work another seven years for Rachel. By the end of the marriage feast Jacob obtained two wives, the second however was to be paid for over another seven years. Through this double marriage and the two concubines Jacob's 12 sons were born. God did not approve of these marriages, but He simply overruled the errors of men for these could not defeat the divine purpose.

It was for this kind of behavior rooted in self-serving that the Lord called Abraham to separate from his family in

Haran. It was for this same reason that Abraham prohibited Isaac from returning to this location to find a wife. Jacob had chosen his own course in deceiving his father and without prayerful consideration returned to Haran out of necessity to avoid being murdered. Had Jacob not deceived his father, the Lord would have brought Rachel to Jacob in his own time without having him return to Haran and his posterity would still have come to number twelve. Had Jacob's sons been raised in a loving selfless home with a single mother, a single set of rules their characters would have been very different.

This history is recorded to demonstrate the starting point of a family downfall. A single mother and father with a single set of selfless values is God's ideal. Fragmentation of the nuclear family unit occurs when one or both parties are self-serving. It also serves as a reminder as to the dangers of associating with those in the world even if they have a religious persona. A heart that is untouched by the Holy Spirit only answers to itself.

CHAPTER 27

JACOB'S DYSFUNCTIONAL FAMILY

Reuben, Simeon, Levi, Judah with wife Leah

"[29] And Laban gave to Rachel his daughter Bilhah his handmaid to be her maid. [30] And he went in also unto Rachel, and he loved also Rachel more than Leah, and served with him yet seven other years. [31] And when the LORD saw that Leah was hated, he opened her womb: but Rachel was barren.

[32] And Leah conceived, and bare a son, and she called his name Reuben: for she said, Surely the LORD hath looked upon my affliction; now therefore my husband will love me. [33] And she conceived again, and bare a son; and said, Because the LORD hath heard I was hated, he hath therefore given me this son also: and she called his name Simeon.

[34] And she conceived again, and bare a son; and said, Now this time will my husband be joined unto me, because I have born him three sons: therefore was his name called Levi. [35] And she conceived again, and bare a son: and she said, Now will I praise the LORD: therefore she called his name Judah; and left bearing." Genesis 29:29-35

Leah was "hated," which simply means she was loved less than her sister. God delayed Rachel from conceiving and blessed Leah with conception for God sought to foster love in Jacobs's heart for Leah. Thus, while Jacob loved Rachel, he was led to appreciate Leah and to deal with her kindly as one of God's daughters.

In many respects the names of the children reflected the state of mind of the wives and their rivalry. Leah's first son was called Reuben which means "to see" as God had seen her predicament. A year later she conceived another son calling him Simeon meaning "hearing," indicating that God had heard her cries. The third son born was called Levi meaning "joined to" in the hope that her husband would indeed become attached to her.

With the birth of her fourth son, she cried: "Now will I praise the LORD" as if she knew that through this son the promised Messiah would come. Thus, she called his name "Judah" the "praised one." Leah's joy was complete. Thus, Jacob came to appreciate her as the mother of his four sons.

Dan and Naphtali with Surrogate Bilhah

"[1] **And when Rachel saw that she bare Jacob no children, Rachel envied her sister; and said unto Jacob, Give me children, or else I die. [2] And Jacob's anger was kindled against Rachel: and he said, Am I in God's stead, who hath withheld from thee the fruit of the womb? [3] And she said, Behold my maid Bilhah, go in unto her; and she shall bear upon my knees, that I may also have children by her.**

[4] **And she gave him Bilhah her handmaid to wife: and Jacob went in unto her. [5] And Bilhah conceived, and bare Jacob a son. [6] And Rachel said, God hath judged me, and hath also heard my voice, and hath given me a son: therefore called she his name Dan. [7] And Bilhah Rachel's maid conceived again, and bare Jacob a second son. [8] And Rachel said, With great wrestlings have I wrestled with my sister, and I have prevailed: and she**

called his name Naphtali." Genesis 30:1-8.

Rachel was jealous of her sister's success and complained to Jacob, "give me children," even though they were just recently married. Sarah waited 25 years for Isaac and Rebekah 20 years before the birth of her twins. Jacobs's answer to her "Am I in God's stead?" was irritable and showed a lack of selflessness. Their disappointment and frustration should have been brought to God in prayer but living amongst idolaters they had not made it a habit to confide in God.

Rachel's proposal that Jacob take her servant Bilhah, was as sinful as when Sarah suggested to Abraham that he take Hagar to be his wife. Sarah's excuse was that there was no heir. Here there was no excuse at all other than jealousy over her sister. God never ordained this behavior, but he overruled it for the purpose of developing the seed of Israel. The arm of God is not short and is certainly not dependent on the schemes and devices of man.

Rachel called her first son through her concubine, Dan, which means "judge." Rachel had considered her sterility as an injustice in view of Leah's fertility. She looked upon the birth of Dan as a divine exoneration and therefore she announced, "God has procured for me justice." The second son born to Rachel by her surrogate Bilhah she now called Naphtali stating, "With great wrestling's."

Gad and Asher with Surrogate Zilppah

"⁹ When Leah saw that she had left bearing, she took Zilpah her maid, and gave her Jacob to wife. ¹⁰ And Zilpah Leah's maid bare Jacob a son. ¹¹ And Leah said, A troop cometh: and she called his name Gad. ¹² And

194

Zilpah Leah's maid bare Jacob a second son. [13] And Leah said, Happy am I, for the daughters will call me blessed: and she called his name Asher." Genesis 30:9-13.

Leah had born one son a year and now after a period of being barren she became a victim of self-pity and resorted to the same human strategies as her sister. She now proposed to have more children from her handmaid Zilpah. According to ancient historical records this practice of surrogacy was considered socially acceptable and for this reason neither Abraham nor Jacob saw any great wrong in their conduct.

Zilpah now produced another son for Leah to which she cried "a troop cometh" an expression that means "in good fortune." The second son of Zilpah was called "Asher" which means "the happy one" or "bringer of happiness."

"[14] And Reuben went in the days of wheat harvest, and found mandrakes in the field, and brought them unto his mother Leah. Then Rachel said to Leah, Give me, I pray thee, of thy son's mandrakes. [15] And she said unto her, Is it a small matter that thou hast taken my husband? and wouldest thou take away my son's mandrakes also? And Rachel said, Therefore he shall lie with thee to night for thy son's mandrakes.

[16] And Jacob came out of the field in the evening, and Leah went out to meet him, and said, Thou must come in unto me; for surely I have hired thee with my son's mandrakes. And he lay with her that night." Genesis 30:14-16.

Reuben, the firstborn son of Jacob and Leah now went out into the field and gathered some mandrakes for his mother, an herb thought to promote fertility. Rachel then asked if she could have some in the hope that she might become more fertile. Leah was angered at the thought of giving her sister something that would increase her chances of conception thus robbing her further of the love and affection of Jacob. Rachel had more faith in the medicinal properties of mandrakes than in the power of God.

From this interchange of words, it appears that Jacob slept most nights with Rachel since she was the favored. Rachel now permits Jacob to spend the night with Leah in exchange for some mandrakes. Leah approaches Jacob as he comes from the field telling him that his work is not over, and he is permitted to be with her that night for she had secured him by the sale of the mandrakes.

Issachar, Zebulun, Dinah with Wife Leah

"[17] **And God hearkened unto Leah, and she conceived, and bare Jacob the fifth son. [18] And Leah said, God hath given me my hire, because I have given my maiden to my husband: and she called his name Issachar. [19] And Leah conceived again, and bare Jacob the sixth son. [20] And Leah said, God hath endued me with a good dowry; now will my husband dwell with me, because I have born him six sons: and she called his name Zebulun. [21] And afterwards she bare a daughter, and called her name Dinah." Genesis 30:17-21.**

Leah now had a fifth son of her body whom she called "Issachar" saying "God hearkened unto me" indicating that it was not from the medicinal properties of the mandrakes but from God Himself. But she saw this as a gift because she had given her husband "unselfishly" to her maid. These two sisters came from families raised in Babylonia, their selfish desires and actions are nauseating.

This family chaos is so typical of our society today and stems from a fragmentation of the nuclear family unit, a unit of two selfless parents governed by a selfless God. These words are a caution to those believers who think they can unite with those of the world with impunity. The self-serving contentious wives and concubines made the life of Jacob miserable. What a contrast between the quiet tent life of his father Isaac, "⁶⁷ And Isaac brought her into his mother Sarah's tent, and took Rebekah, and she became his wife; and he loved her: and Isaac was comforted after his mother's death." Genesis 24:67.

Leah now gave birth to a sixth son, which she named Zebulun, which means "dwelling." Here Leah expressed the hope that Jacob would now prefer her over Rachael and would now dwell with her in the honored relationship of the first wife. Leah also bore Jacob one daughter, Dinah, this was to be Jacob's first and only daughter.

Jospeh and Benjamin with Wife Rachael

"**²² And God remembered Rachel, and God hearkened to her, and opened her womb.²³ And she conceived, and bare a son; and said, God hath taken away my reproach:²⁴ And she called his name Joseph; and said, The LORD shall add to me another son." Genesis 30:22-24.**

Rachel finally took the matter to the Lord in prayer, and she conceived her first-born son. What impatience, unbelief and human devising could not obtain she now obtained by faith. In the ancient times, a barren woman was despised and was considered a shame and a curse. Amongst the Jews barrenness would justify divorce or polygamy. God now had heard her "reproach." Her first son she called "Joseph" which means, "he takes away," a reference to her reproach. Jacob's 11 sons were born in Haran, his 12th son Benjamin, was born to Rachel in the land of promise.

CHAPTER 28

JACOB PROSPERS AND DEPARTS HARAN

"^{25} And it came to pass, when Rachel had born Joseph, that Jacob said unto Laban, Send me away, that I may go unto mine own place, and to my country. ^{26} Give me my wives and my children, for whom I have served thee, and let me go: for thou knowest my service which I have done thee. ^{27} And Laban said unto him, I pray thee, if I have found favour in thine eyes, tarry: for I have learned by experience that the LORD hath blessed me for thy sake. ^{28} And he said, Appoint me thy wages, and I will give it...

^{31} And he said, What shall I give thee? And Jacob said, Thou shalt not give me any thing: if thou wilt do this thing for me, I will again feed and keep thy flock: ^{32} I will pass through all thy flock to day, removing from thence all the speckled and spotted cattle, and all the brown cattle among the sheep, and the spotted and speckled among the goats: and of such shall be my hire." Genesis 30:25-32.

Toward the end of the seven years in which Jacob was required to work for Rachel's hand, Rachel gave birth to Joseph. Jacob now asked Laban for permission to return to Canaan but Laban not wanting to lose such a hard worker asked him to "name his price." This, however, did not stop Laban from changing his wages 10 times in 6 years (Genesis 31: 7).

Jacob now proposed that for payment Laban would give him all the mixed colored animals from his herds. Laban's sons would attend Jacobs's mixed colored animals and

Jacob would attend Laban's pure colored animals. Laban did not count on the recessive genes of animals in which a pure colored animal might give birth to an animal that was mixed in color (Genesis 30:25-36).

Jacob, however, tried to influence the color of the solid-colored animals in his care by exposing these animals to branches that had been peeled in part of their bark giving the branches a speckled appearance. The idea was that Laban's pure colored animals would see the speckled colored rods while mating and this would somehow influence their offspring to become speckled which would then become Jacobs. (Genesis 30:37-43).

"[3] **And the LORD said unto Jacob, Return unto the land of thy fathers, and to thy kindred; and I will be with thee. [4] And Jacob sent and called Rachel and Leah to the field unto his flock, [5]And said unto them, I see your father's countenance, that it is not toward me as before; but the God of my father hath been with me.[6] And ye know that with all my power I have served your father. [7] And your father hath deceived me, and changed my wages ten times; but God suffered him not to hurt me...**

[14] **And Rachel and Leah answered and said unto him, Is there yet any portion or inheritance for us in our father's house? [15] Are we not counted of him strangers? for he hath sold us, and hath quite devoured also our money. [16] For all the riches which God hath taken from our father, that is ours, and our children's: now then, whatsoever God hath said unto thee, do." Genesis 31:3-7, 14-16.**

"17 Then Jacob rose up, and set his sons and his wives upon camels;18 And he carried away all his cattle, and all his goods which he had gotten, the cattle of his getting, which he had gotten in Padanaram, for to go to Isaac his father in the land of Canaan.

19 And Laban went to shear his sheep: and Rachel had stolen the images that were her father's.20 And Jacob stole away unawares to Laban the Syrian, in that he told him not that he fled.21 So he fled with all that he had; and he rose up, and passed over the river, and set his face toward the mount Gilead.22 And it was told Laban on the third day that Jacob was fled.23 And he took his brethren with him, and pursued after him seven days' journey; and they overtook him in the mount Gilead." Genesis 31:17-22.

While Laban was away sheering his sheep the entire family with all their possessions set out on the homeward journey. Rachel before leaving stole the figurines of her father's gods which in accordance with ancient custom the possessor was entitled to inherit their father's estate. Hearing of their departure Laban set out in pursuit, but the Lord appeared to him in a dream instructing him not to harm Jacob (Genesis 31:24).

On reaching Jacob about ten days later Laban assumes the role of the good natured but grievously wronged and deeply hurt father. Laban accuses Jacob of stealing his family gods and accordingly begins to search Jacob's tents. Rachel who had stolen the gods hid them under some camel furniture on which she sat stating she could not move for she was menstruating. Laban now proposes a pact of friendship, and the men depart amicably. Thus, the word of

God spoken at Bethel to bring Jacob back to the Promised Land was in the process of fulfillment. (Genesis 31:22-55)

CHAPTER 29

JACOB'S NAME CHANGED TO ISRAEL

"¹ And Jacob went on his way, and the angels of God met him.² And when Jacob saw them, he said, This is God's host: and he called the name of that place Mahanaim.

³ And Jacob sent messengers before him to Esau his brother unto the land of Seir, the country of Edom. ⁴ And he commanded them, saying, Thus shall ye speak unto my lord Esau; Thy servant Jacob saith thus, I have sojourned with Laban, and stayed there until now: ⁵ And I have oxen, and asses, flocks, and menservants, and womenservants: and I have sent to tell my lord, that I may find grace in thy sight." Genesis 32:3-5.

Mahanaim, meaning "double host" is a reference to the two bands of angels accompanying him, one band before him the other behind. These angels were the assurance of God's protection in his anticipated meeting with Esau. Jacob now sends messengers to disarm the prejudices of Esau by having them address Esau as "my lord" and referring to Jacob as "thy servant Jacob." Jacob references his wealth indicating that his return is not to collect on their father's inheritance.

"⁶ And the messengers returned to Jacob, saying, We came to thy brother Esau, and also he cometh to meet thee, and four hundred men with him.⁷ Then Jacob was greatly afraid and distressed: and he divided the people that was with him, and the flocks, and herds, and the camels, into two bands; ⁸ And said, If Esau come to the one company, and smite it, then the other company which is left shall escape.

⁹ And Jacob said, O God of my father Abraham, and God of my father Isaac, the LORD which saidst unto me, Return unto thy country, and to thy kindred, and I will deal well with thee:¹⁰ I am not worthy of the least of all the mercies, and of all the truth, which thou hast shewed unto thy servant; for with my staff I passed over this Jordan; and now I am become two bands.

¹¹ Deliver me, I pray thee, from the hand of my brother, from the hand of Esau: for I fear him, lest he will come and smite me, and the mother with the children.¹² And thou saidst, I will surely do thee good, and make thy seed as the sand of the sea, which cannot be numbered for multitude." Genesis 32:6-12.

Despite the promise of angelic protection which at this point evidently faded from his sight, Jacob became fearful. Jacob's company consisted of unarmed women and children. He decides to divide the company into two groups, in the event of an attack at least one company would escape. Doing all he can he now turns to God in prayer recalling the promises of God to become a great nation through whom the Messiah would come.

" ¹³ And he lodged there that same night; and took of that which came to his hand a present for Esau his brother;¹⁴ Two hundred she goats, and twenty he goats, two hundred ewes, and twenty rams,¹⁵ Thirty milch camels with their colts, forty kine, and ten bulls, twenty she asses, and ten foals.¹⁶ And he delivered them into the hand of his servants, every drove by themselves; and said unto his servants, Pass over before me, and put a space betwixt drove and drove.¹⁷ And he commanded the foremost, saying, When Esau my brother meeteth thee, and asketh thee, saying, Whose art thou? and whither goest thou? and whose are these before thee?[18] Then thou shalt say, They be thy servant Jacob's; it is a present sent unto my lord Esau: and, behold, also he is behind us.

[19] And so commanded he the second, and the third, and all that followed the droves, saying, On this manner shall ye speak unto Esau, when ye find him.[20] And say ye moreover, Behold, thy servant Jacob is behind us. For he said, I will appease him with the present that goeth before me, and afterward I will see his face; peradventure he will accept of me." Genesis 32:13-20.

Jacob now relies once again on self by several droves of animals to Esau in the hope that his heart will be softened. The droves were sent at different intervals designed to have a cumulative effect; it more difficult to reject several gifts of kindness than one gift alone.

"[21] So went the present over before him: and himself lodged that night in the company.[22] And he rose up that night, and took his two wives, and his two womenservants, and his eleven sons, and passed over the ford Jabbok.[23] And he took them, and sent them over the brook, and sent over that he had." Genesis 32: 21-23.

Having received no word from God nor any positive affirmation of his gifts, Jacob becomes desperate. Relying again on self for the safety of his family, he now sends his family over the river Jabbok, himself remaining behind to confront Esau.

When we are in crisis the Lord often does not answer us immediately that He might teach us to trust fully in His selfless providence since all relationships are based upon trust. Jacob's grandfather, Abraham, was willing to sacrifice Isaac believing God would resurrect him from the dead, but this experience was to become his own. Had he believed God, he would have faced the slaughter believing God would interpose or would resurrect his family as God had promised the proliferation of his seed.

"**²⁴ And Jacob was left alone; and there wrestled a man with him until the breaking of the day." Genesis 32:24**

This struggle that is so natural to the human heart, the struggle between relying on a Selfless God (faith) versus relying on the strength of self (unbelief) begins to unfold in a real-life confrontation with a supposed assailant.

"**²⁵ And when he saw that he prevailed not against him, he touched the hollow of his thigh; and the hollow of Jacob's thigh was out of joint, as he wrestled with him.²⁶ And he said, Let me go, for the day breaketh. And he said, I will not let thee go, except thou bless me." Genesis 32:25, 26.**

Jacob evidently realized the one he was struggling with was not an aggressor, but God (vs 30) - the angel of the Lord. He clung so tight to the fight until he was broken by the dislocation of his thigh. This represented the breaking of self-reliance.

The gospel was initially preached to Jacob in a dream of the ladder reaching down to earth. At the time he did not realize this was Christ but simply an unobstructed channel between God and man. Now the gospel is opened further to his view in this physical struggle with that very ladder, the angel of the Lord. "[44] And whosoever shall fall on this stone shall be broken: but on whomsoever it shall fall, it will grind him to powder." Mathew 21:44. Jacob refused to be ground to powder and he clung to Christ pleading for a blessing. In this fight Jacob fell on the rock and was broken, self-reliance was defeated! Hence forth his trust in a selfless God was perfected.

"[27] And he said unto him, What is thy name? And he said, Jacob.[28] And he said, Thy name shall be called no more Jacob, but Israel: for as a prince hast thou power with God and with men, and hast prevailed.[29] And Jacob asked him, and said, Tell me, I pray thee, thy name. And he said, Wherefore is it that thou dost ask after my name? And he blessed him there.[30] And Jacob called the name of the place Peniel: for I have seen God face to face, and my life is preserved." Genesis 32: 27-30.

Jacob realized he was struggling with Christ: "for I have seen God face to face" (vs. 30). The prophet Hosea refers to the assailant as an angel (Hosea 12:3,4), thus the assailant was none other than the angel of the LORD, Jesus Christ himself. For some it is difficult to imagine Christ who is depicted in the New Testament as a "man of sorrows and acquainted with grief" (Isaiah 53:3), as the mighty Commander of the armies of heaven. Jacob now named the place "Peniel," which means "the face of God," for he had seen God face-to-face and lived.

This physical battle is representative of the struggle of the heart and re-defined Jacob's experience with God. The honored name change to Israel was henceforth to memorialize the night of struggle between faith (trusting in a selfless God) and unbelief (trusting in self). The name was to be transmitted first to his literal descendants and later to his spiritual descendants. All who claim to be descendants of spiritual Israel will have this experience of falling on the rock and being broken of SELF RELIANCE and in turn become trusting and reliant on a SELFLESS GOD, who knows all and sees all and acts in the best interest of the universe at large.

"[1] **And Jacob lifted up his eyes, and looked, and, behold, Esau came, and with him four hundred men. And he divided the children unto Leah, and unto Rachel, and unto the two handmaids.[2] And he put the handmaids and their children foremost, and Leah and her children after, and Rachel and Joseph hindermost.[3] And he passed over before them, and bowed himself to the ground seven times, until he came near to his brother.[4] And Esau ran to meet him, and embraced him, and fell on his neck, and kissed him: and they wept." Genesis 33:1-4.**

CHAPTER 30

JACOB'S RETURN TO CANAAN

Murder at Shechem

"**¹⁸ And Jacob came to Shalem, a city of Shechem, which is in the land of Canaan, when he came from Padanaram; and pitched his tent before the city. ¹⁹ And he bought a parcel of a field, where he had spread his tent, at the hand of the children of Hamor, Shechem's father, for an hundred pieces of money. ²⁰ And he erected there an altar, and called it EleloheIsrael." Genesis 33:18-20.**

After the meeting with Esau, Jacob settled in Shechem of Canaan and here he erected an altar and called it "EleloheIsrael," interpreted as "The mighty God, is the God of Israel." This altar was a memorial to God's mercy in returning him safely to the land of his fathers after more than 20 years in exile.

"**¹ And Dinah the daughter of Leah, which she bare unto Jacob, went out to see the daughters of the land.² And when Shechem the son of Hamor the Hivite, prince of the country, saw her, he took her, and lay with her, and defiled her…" Genesis 34: 1, 2.**

Jacob's only daughter with his wife Leah, disregarded the provisions of the Lord to remain separate (Deuteronomy 7:2-6. 2 Corinthian's 6: 14-18, 1 Corinthians 5:9-13). Venturing out amongst those of the world, she met a young man and the two engaged in premarital relations.

"⁷ And the sons of Jacob came out of the field when they heard it: and the men were grieved, and they were very wroth, because he had wrought folly in Israel in lying with Jacob's daughter; which thing ought not to be done. ²⁵ ...that two of the sons of Jacob, Simeon and Levi, Dinah's brethren, took each man his sword, and came upon the city boldly, and slew all the males.²⁶ And they slew Hamor and Shechem his son with the edge of the sword, and took Dinah out of Shechem's house, and went out." Genesis 34: 7, 25, 26,

Dinah's two brothers, Simeon and Levi enraged at the disgrace of their sister now executed revenge by murdering all the males of an entire city. All property and life belong to God, He alone is judge and executioner (Hebrews 10:30). Man sees only in part and is not capable of rendering sound judgment.

"²⁷ The sons of Jacob came upon the slain, and spoiled the city, because they had defiled their sister.²⁸ They took their sheep, and their oxen, and their asses, and that which was in the city, and that which was in the field, ²⁹ And all their wealth, and all their little ones, and their wives took they captive, and spoiled even all that was in the house." Genesis 34:27-29.

The disgrace of their sister was not satisfied with the murder of one guilty man and many innocent men, but they felt they were justified in helping themselves like ravenous beasts to the possession and wealth of the slain, their children and their wives. Jacob had prevailed with God in the battle with the Angel of the Lord, but his children had not learned these lessons in selflessness.

"**³⁰ And Jacob said to Simeon and Levi, Ye have troubled me to make me to stink among the inhabitants of the land, among the Canaanites and the Perizzites: and I being few in number, they shall gather themselves together against me, and slay me; and I shall be destroyed, I and my house.³¹ And they said, Should he deal with our sister as with an harlot?" Genesis 34:30, 31.**

On reprimand the answer of Simeon and Levi, like Cain, demonstrated no remorse for their self-serving impulsive actions. Like Cain they failed to gain the mastery over self that like a wild best was lying in wait for an opportunity to strike. They justified their ill acts by the ill acts of another.

Jacob's Blended Family

Dinah and her brothers were raised in a "blended family," multiple parents with multiple children. Such homes have considerable challenges when it comes to discipline as each parent has their own set of rules and different parenting styles resulting in oppositional, strong-willed and defiant children who grow up to demonstrate delinquent and even criminal behaviors.

The 4 basic rules of parenting as per God's example demonstrated in Eden:

1) Clear communication of rules and expectations

   – do not eat of the tree.

2) Clear communication of the consequences

   – eating leads to death.

3) Keeping consistent accountability

   – expulsion from the garden.

4) Discipline in selflessness (love & patience)

   - promise of a redeemer.

The saying "spare the rod, spoil the child" is based upon Proverbs 13:24. "He that spareth his rod hateth his son: but he that loveth him chasteneth him betimes." The rod spoken of here is a symbol of discipline, it is not a literal rod, and this passage does not give sanction to corporal punishment. Consequences for non-compliance with rules can be in the form of a restriction of privileges, not the use of a lash. Lashing out at a child in anger only teaches the child that aggression is the solution to conflict resolution.

From the behavior of Jacobs's children, we can infer his parenting was lax, there were few rules and those that did exist were seldom enforced and those that were enforced were likely done so in anger and aggression. Self-serving ignores good parenting, it does not welcome the conflict that is generated when children are held accountable for their actions. Self prefers the easy road of permissive parenting on the one hand or a dictatorial style of parenting on the other hand where rules are generated that are not in the best interest of the child and are enforced without love and tenderness.

Jacob's Recommitment at Bethel

"[1] And God said unto Jacob, Arise, go up to Bethel, and dwell there: and make there an altar unto God, that appeared unto thee when thou fleddest from the face of Esau thy brother." Genesis 35:1

Jacob was now to leave Shechem and return to Bethel, the location where he rested the first night after deceiving his father decades before. Here he had the dream of the ladder spanning between heaven and earth with the angels ascending and descending on the ladder.

On waking from the dream Jacob devoted himself to walking in the path of selflessness, here began his sanctification. Jacob's return to Bethel was to show him that God's promise was fulfilled in returning him safely to the land of Canaan, but Jacob was to renew his promise of selflessness not for himself only but now for his whole family.

"² Then Jacob said unto his household, and to all that were with him, Put away the strange gods that are among you, and be clean, and change your garments: ³ And let us arise, and go up to Bethel; and I will make there an altar unto God, who answered me in the day of my distress…" Genesis 35: 2, 3.

Jacob now calls his family to put away the "strange gods," that is anything that fosters the spirit of self-serving and cleanse themselves and change their clothes, for Jacob this outward cleansing was symbolic of an inward cleansing.

"⁴ And they gave unto Jacob all the strange gods which were in their hand, and all their earrings which were in their ears; and Jacob hid them under the oak which was by Shechem. ⁵ And they journeyed: and the terror of God was upon the cities that were round about them, and they did not pursue after the sons of Jacob." Genesis 35:4, 5.

The Death of Rachael

"**¹⁶ And they journeyed from Bethel; and there was but a little way to come to Ephrath: and Rachel travailed, and she had hard labour. ¹⁸ And it came to pass, as her soul was in departing, (for she died) that she called his name Benoni: but his father called him Benjamin. ¹⁹ And Rachel died, and was buried in the way to Ephrath, which is Bethlehem.." Genesis 35:16-21.**

Rachel as she lay dying in childbirth called her son "Benoni" which means "son of my sorrow," but Jacob changed his name to "Benjamin," "son of my right hand." This name was to be an expression of hope, a reminder of the joy of his twelfth son rather than a memory of the loss of his wife. Why this young mother was laid so early in the grave we will not know, perhaps to spare her from the grief of seeing her son Joseph being sold into Egypt. But it is certain that the mysteries of providence that seem so dark to us will one day be made clear in heaven.

SECTION VI
JOSEPH IN EGYPT

CHAPTER 31

JOSEPH SOLD INTO EGYPT

Jacob's Poor Parenting

"**¹ And Jacob dwelt in the land wherein his father was a stranger, in the land of Canaan. ² These are the generations of Jacob. Joseph, being seventeen years old, was feeding the flock with his brethren; and the lad was with the sons of Bilhah, and with the sons of Zilpah, his father's wives: and Joseph brought unto his father their evil report." Genesis 37:1, 2**

Jacob and his sons lived in the countryside of Canaan. Joseph, being the second youngest evidently accompanied his older brothers as they attended the flocks. The scriptures state that Joseph reported his brother's evil deeds to his father, and for this reason they hated him. "Tattletale" behavior is a self-righteous behavior, it's a behavior that makes one feel good and look better by highlighting the shortcomings of others. Had Joseph not been his favorite, Jacob would have placed this behavior in check.

"**³ Now Israel loved Joseph more than all his children, because he was the son of his old age: and he made him a coat of many colours. ⁴ And when his brethren saw that their father loved him more than all his brethren, they hated him, and could not speak peaceably unto him." Genesis 37:3,4.**

Jacobs's favoritism over Joseph in making him a special robe of many colors only triggered the anger of his brothers. Jacob's mother Rebekah showed him preferential treatment, Jacob showed preferential treatment to Rachel and now again he showed preferential treatment to Joseph. Favoritism is rooted in self and causes division. While the father may have intended this special robe for his son, he would have done well to make one for each of his sons.

"⁵ And Joseph dreamed a dream, and he told it his brethren: and they hated him yet the more.⁶ And he said unto them, Hear, I pray you, this dream which I have dreamed:⁷ For, behold, we were binding sheaves in the field, and, lo, my sheaf arose, and also stood upright; and, behold, your sheaves stood round about, and made obeisance to my sheaf. ⁸ And his brethren said to him, Shalt thou indeed reign over us? or shalt thou indeed have dominion over us? And they hated him yet the more for his dreams, and for his words.

⁹ And he dreamed yet another dream, and told it his brethren, and said, Behold, I have dreamed a dream more; and, behold, the sun and the moon and the eleven stars made obeisance to me. ¹⁰ And he told it to his father, and to his brethren: and his father rebuked him, and said unto him, What is this dream that thou hast dreamed? Shall I and thy mother and thy brethren indeed come to bow down ourselves to thee to the earth? ¹¹ And his brethren envied him; but his father observed the saying." Genesis 37:5-9.

Had Joseph not been a "tattletale" and a father's favorite these two dreams may have been simply dismissed by his brothers as mere dreams or a warning from the Lord but instead they triggered the ravenous beast of "self" lurking within to a frenzy of jealousy and hatred.

"12 And his brethren went to feed their father's flock in Shechem…. 18 And when they saw him afar off, even before he came near unto them, they conspired against him to slay him.19 And they said one to another, Behold, this dreamer cometh.20 Come now therefore, and let us slay him, and cast him into some pit, and we will say, Some evil beast hath devoured him: and we shall see what will become of his dreams. 21 And Reuben … said, Let us not kill him.22 And Reuben said unto them, Shed no blood, but cast him into this pit that is in the wilderness, and lay no hand upon him; that he might rid him out of their hands, to deliver him to his father again." Genesis 37:12, 18-22.

Jacob, concerned about the location of his sons and his flocks, sent Joseph in search of them. While yet in the distance the brothers saw his approach and plotted to kill him. Reuben, the oldest brother now opposed the plan and suggested to throw Joseph into a pit with the secret hope of rescuing him later. Had he been selfless, Joseph would have been spared but Reuben was "unstable as water" (Genesis 49:4), spineless and desired to be liked by everyone.

"23 And it came to pass, when Joseph was come unto his brethren, that they stript Joseph out of his coat, …24 And they took him, and cast him into a pit: …25 And they sat down to eat bread: and they lifted up their eyes and looked, and, behold, a company of Ishmeelites came from Gilead ….28 …and they drew and lifted up Joseph out of the pit, and sold Joseph to the Ishmeelites for twenty pieces of silver: and they brought Joseph into Egypt.

31 And they took Joseph's coat, and killed a kid of the goats, and dipped the coat in the blood; 32 And they sent

the coat of many colours, and they brought it to their father; and said, This have we found: know now whether it be thy son's coat or no.[33] And he knew it, and said, It is my son's coat; an evil beast hath devoured him; Joseph is without doubt rent in pieces. [34] And Jacob rent his clothes, and put sackcloth upon his loins, and mourned for his son many days." Genesis 37:23-25, 31-34.

As a company of Ishmaelite's passed by, Joseph was pulled out of the pit and sold. The scene of his agonizing cries on deaf ears is now only a subject of the imagination. Reuben, who was evidently not present during the sale, was distraught on finding Joseph missing. The brothers then conceived a plan to deceive their father into believing Joseph had been killed by a wild animal. They certainly did not care to witness the utter abandonment of grief experienced by their father, who "refused to be comforted."

Divine providence over-ruled the murderous designs of Joseph's self-serving brothers. The caravan of Ishmaelite's coming at this precise time was heaven's means of saving the life of Joseph from his brothers. This in turn became a means by which their lives were also to be saved. This life experience of Joseph changed the once coddled child into a man overnight. The experiences that he passed through from the time he was sold into Egypt worked to purify his character. "[10] For it became him, for whom are all things, and by whom are all things, in bringing many sons unto glory, to make the captain of their salvation perfect through sufferings." Hebrews 2:10.

CHAPTER 32

JOSEPH'S INCARCERATION

"¹ **And Joseph was brought down to Egypt; and Potiphar, an officer of Pharaoh, captain of the guard, an Egyptian, bought him of the hands of the Ishmeelites, which had brought him down thither.**

² **And the LORD was with Joseph, and he was a prosperous man; and he was in the house of his master the Egyptian.³ And his master saw that the LORD was with him, and that the LORD made all that he did to prosper in his hand... ⁶ And he left all that he had in Joseph's hand; and he knew not ought he had, save the bread which he did eat. And Joseph was a goodly person, and well favoured." Genesis 38:1-3, 6.**

Joseph was a despised slave in a heathen land and despite this he performed all his duties and responsibilities as though unto the Lord. In all that Joseph did the Lord blessed his efforts, even his idolatrous earthly master credited his success to the God of Israel. The example of Joseph is a lesson for youth today and an example that parents may point to when teaching their children diligence and responsibility in all their chores.

"⁷ **And it came to pass after these things, that his master's wife cast her eyes upon Joseph; and she said, Lie with me.⁸ But he refused, and said unto his master's wife, Behold, my master wotteth not what is with me in the house, and he hath committed all that he hath to my hand;⁹ There is none greater in this house than I; neither hath he kept back any thing from me but thee, because thou art his wife: how then can I do this great**

wickedness, and sin against God?" Genesis 39:7-9

Joseph had gained Potipher's trust and was accordingly set as caretaker over his estate. While going about his daily duties Potiphar's wife made a sexual advance toward him but he declined her advances not wanting to sin against God nor betray his master's trust. The Law of God is framed in selflessness to prevent harm, taking another man's wife would cause great harm to the marriage.

"¹⁰ And it came to pass, as she spake to Joseph day by day, that he hearkened not unto her, to lie by her, or to be with her.¹¹ And it came to pass about this time, that Joseph went into the house to do his business; and there was none of the men of the house there within.¹² And she caught him by his garment, saying, Lie with me: and he left his garment in her hand, and fled, and got him out ...

¹⁹ And it came to pass, when his master heard the words of his wife, which she spake unto him, saying, After this manner did thy servant to me; that his wrath was kindled. ²⁰ And Joseph's master took him, and put him into the prison, a place where the king's prisoners were bound: and he was there in the prison." Genesis 39:10-12, 19, 20.

On one occasion Potiphar's wife found herself alone in the home without any attendants and she again made an advance on the young Hebrew. Joseph fled the scene of temptation leaving behind an article of his clothing in her hand. Potiphar's wife, feeling herself scorned now accused Joseph of the very act, which she herself had suggested. Joseph was now imprisoned. (Genesis 39:13-29).

Joseph Interprets Two Dreams

"²¹ But the LORD was with Joseph, and shewed him mercy, and gave him favour in the sight of the keeper of the prison.²² And the keeper of the prison committed to Joseph's hand all the prisoners that were in the prison; and whatsoever they did there, he was the doer of it.²³ The keeper of the prison looked not to any thing that was under his hand; because the LORD was with him, and that which he did, the LORD made it to prosper."
Genesis 39:21-23

"¹ And it came to pass after these things, that the butler of the king of Egypt and his baker had offended their lord the king of Egypt.² And Pharaoh was wroth against two of his officers, against the chief of the butlers, and against the chief of the bakers.³ And he put them in ward in the house of the captain of the guard, into the prison, the place where Joseph was bound."
Genesis 40:1-3.

The butler (cupbearer) and baker were responsible for ensuring the safety of the King's food and drink from poison. There was likely some attempt to assassinate the king and pending an investigation both men were incarcerated. While in jail they had dreams which Joseph was asked to interpret.

"⁹ And the chief butler told his dream to Joseph, and said to him, In my dream, behold, a vine was before me; ¹⁰ And in the vine were three branches: and it was as though it budded, and her blossoms shot forth; and the clusters thereof brought forth ripe grapes:¹¹ And Pharaoh's cup was in my hand: and I took the grapes, and pressed them into Pharaoh's cup, and I gave the cup into Pharaoh's hand.

[12] And Joseph said unto him, This is the interpretation of it: The three branches are three days: [13] Yet within three days shall Pharaoh lift up thine head, and restore thee unto thy place: and thou shalt deliver Pharaoh's cup into his hand, after the former manner when thou wast his butler...

[16] When the chief baker saw that the interpretation was good, he said unto Joseph, I also was in my dream, and, behold, I had three white baskets on my head: [17] And in the uppermost basket there was of all manner of bakemeats for Pharaoh; and the birds did eat them out of the basket upon my head.

[18] And Joseph answered and said, This is the interpretation thereof: The three baskets are three days: [19] Yet within three days shall Pharaoh lift up thy head from off thee, and shall hang thee on a tree; and the birds shall eat thy flesh from off thee.

[20] And it came to pass the third day, which was Pharaoh's birthday,... [21] And he restored the chief butler unto his butlership again;...: [22] But he hanged the chief baker: as Joseph had interpreted to them. [23] Yet did not the chief butler remember Joseph, but forgat him." Genesis 40:9-13, 16-23.

CHAPTER 33

JOSEPH AS GOVERNOR OF EGYPT

"[1] And it came to pass at the end of two full years, that Pharaoh dreamed: and, behold, he stood by the river. [2] And, behold, there came up out of the river seven well favoured kine and fatfleshed; and they fed in a meadow. [3] And, behold, seven other kine came up after them out of the river, ill favoured and leanfleshed; and stood by the other kine upon the brink of the river. [4] And the ill favoured and leanfleshed kine did eat up the seven well favoured and fat kine. So Pharaoh awoke.

[5] And he slept and dreamed the second time: and, behold, seven ears of corn came up upon one stalk, rank and good. [6] And, behold, seven thin ears and blasted with the east wind sprung up after them. [7] And the seven thin ears devoured the seven rank and full ears. And Pharaoh awoke, and, behold, it was a dream." Genesis 41:1-7.

Pharaoh dreamed two dreams; in the first he saw seven well-fed cattle being consumed by seven lean cattle. In the second dream he saw seven healthy ears of corn being consumed by seven ears of sickly corn. The following morning Pharaoh called upon the magicians to interpret his dreams, but they were unable to do so. The butler remembering Joseph in prison recounts to Pharaoh how Joseph correctly interpreted his own dream and that of the baker. Joseph was subsequently summoned before Pharaoh to interpret the dream.

"[25] And Joseph said unto Pharaoh, The dream of Pharaoh is one: God hath shewed Pharaoh what he is about to do.[26] The seven good kine are seven years; and the seven good ears are seven years: the dream is one.[27] And the seven thin and ill favoured kine that came up after them are seven years; and the seven empty ears blasted with the east wind shall be seven years of famine.

[28] This is the thing which I have spoken unto Pharaoh: What God is about to do he sheweth unto Pharaoh.[29] Behold, there come seven years of great plenty throughout all the land of Egypt:[30] And there shall arise after them seven years of famine; and all the plenty shall be forgotten in the land of Egypt; and the famine shall consume the land;[31] And the plenty shall not be known in the land by reason of that famine following; for it shall be very grievous. [32] And for that the dream was doubled unto Pharaoh twice; it is because the thing is established by God, and God will shortly bring it to pass." Genesis 41:25-32.

Pharaoh now recounts the dreams and Joseph gives the interpretation that seven years of plenty would be followed by seven years of drought. The dream is repeated using different symbolism to indicate this was not a random dream.

"[33] Now therefore let Pharaoh look out a man discreet and wise, and set him over the land of Egypt... [39] And Pharaoh said unto Joseph, Forasmuch as God hath shewed thee all this, there is none so discreet and wise as thou art: [40] Thou shalt be over my house, and according unto thy word shall all my people be ruled: only in the throne will I be greater than thou... [43] And he made him to ride in the second chariot which he had; and they cried before him, Bow the knee: and he made him ruler over all the land of Egypt." Genesis 41:33, 39, 40, 43.

Joseph was now entrusted with preparing for the coming famine and he carefully amassed and stored food to the point they had lost count. He was second in authority in Egypt next to Pharaoh alone, riding in a chariot to which all men bowed. Surely the dream he had of his brother's sheaves bowing before his sheaf and the dream of the sun, moon and stars bowing before him so many years before came to remembrance.

"[46] And Joseph was thirty years old when he stood before Pharaoh king of Egypt. And Joseph went out from the presence of Pharaoh, and went throughout all the land of Egypt. [47] And in the seven plenteous years the earth brought forth by handfuls. [48] And he gathered up all the food of the seven years, which were in the land of Egypt, and laid up the food in the cities: the food of the field, which was round about every city, laid he up in the same. [49] And Joseph gathered corn as the sand of the sea, very much, until he left numbering; for it was without number.

[50] And unto Joseph were born two sons before the years of famine came, which Asenath the daughter of Potipherah priest of On bare unto him. [51] And Joseph called the name of the firstborn Manasseh: For God, said he, hath made me forget all my toil, and all my father's house. [52]And the name of the second called he Ephraim: For God hath caused me to be fruitful in the land of my affliction." Genesis 41:46-52

Joseph spent a total of thirteen years as a slave, for the divine record declares he was 17 when he was sold into

Egypt (Genesis 37:2) and 30 when he stood before Pharaoh. Joseph bore two sons during the years of plenty; Manasseh which means "causing to forget," for this son helped him to forget the long years of slavery and the longing he had for his father's house. "Ephraim" means, "double fruitful." This was an expression of gratitude for God had given him, who was once a slave, now a happy family with two sons.

CHAPTER 34

JOSEPH TESTS HIS BROTHERS

The First Mission to Egypt

"[56] And the famine was over all the face of the earth: And Joseph opened all the storehouses, and sold unto the Egyptians; and the famine waxed sore in the land of Egypt. [57] And all countries came into Egypt to Joseph for to buy corn; because that the famine was so sore in all lands." Genesis 41:56, 57.

"[1] Now when Jacob saw that there was corn in Egypt, Jacob said unto his sons, Why do ye look one upon another? [2] And he said, Behold, I have heard that there is corn in Egypt: get you down thither, and buy for us from thence; that we may live, and not die.[3] And Joseph's ten brethren went down to buy corn in Egypt.[4] But Benjamin, Joseph's brother, Jacob sent not with his brethren; for he said, Lest peradventure mischief befall him.[5] And the sons of Israel came to buy corn among those that came: for the famine was in the land of Canaan.

[6] And Joseph was the governor over the land, and he it was that sold to all the people of the land: and Joseph's brethren came, and bowed down themselves before him with their faces to the earth.[7] And Joseph saw his brethren, and he knew them, but made himself strange unto them, and spake roughly unto them; and he said unto them, Whence come ye? And they said, From the land of Canaan to buy food.[8] And Joseph knew his brethren, but they knew not him." Genesis 42:1-7.

Jacob now sends his 10 sons down into Egypt to buy food, but he refused to send Benjamin, the only remaining child of his beloved Rachel. Benjamin was a young man around 20 years old. On arriving in Egypt, Joseph's brothers did not recognize him. It had been twenty years since they last saw him, he was older, clean-shaven as opposed to wearing the traditional semitic beard and he spoke to them in the language of Egypt.

"**[9] And Joseph remembered the dreams which he dreamed of them, and said unto them, Ye are spies; to see the nakedness of the land ye are come. [10] And they said unto him, Nay, my lord, but to buy food are thy servants come. [11] We are all one man's sons; we are true men, thy servants are no spies. [12] And he said unto them, Nay, but to see the nakedness of the land ye are come. [13] And they said, Thy servants are twelve brethren, the sons of one man in the land of Canaan; and, behold, the youngest is this day with our father, and one is not. [14] And Joseph said unto them, That is it that I spake unto you, saying, Ye are spies:**

[15] Hereby ye shall be proved: By the life of Pharaoh ye shall not go forth hence, except your youngest brother come hither. [16] Send one of you, and let him fetch your brother, and ye shall be kept in prison, that your words may be proved, whether there be any truth in you: or else by the life of Pharaoh surely ye are spies. [17] And he put them all together into ward three days." Genesis 42:9-17.**

Joseph now accuses his brothers of being spies, not for revenge but to better determine their frame of mind. The fact that Benjamin was missing was certainly concerning to

Joseph, could it be that his younger brother had been murdered or sold? The brothers stated that they were the sons of one man. Joseph now asked proof of their story by bringing their youngest brother to Egypt before they would be supplied with any more food. The brothers refused because they knew that their father would refuse such a request. Joseph accordingly had them incarcerated for three days so that he might further test them. Joseph had suffered in prison for almost 13 years. Now they were to spend only 3 days.

"[18] **And Joseph said unto them the third day, This do, and live; for I fear God:**[19] **If ye be true men, let one of your brethren be bound in the house of your prison: go ye, carry corn for the famine of your houses:** [20] **But bring your youngest brother unto me; so shall your words be verified, and ye shall not die. And they did so.**

"[21] **And they said one to another, We are verily guilty concerning our brother, in that we saw the anguish of his soul, when he besought us, and we would not hear; therefore is this distress come upon us.**[22] **And Reuben answered them, saying, Spake I not unto you, saying, Do not sin against the child; and ye would not hear? therefore, behold, also his blood is required.**[23] **And they knew not that Joseph understood them; for he spake unto them by an interpreter.**[24] **And he turned himself about from them, and wept; and returned to them again, and communed with them, and took from them Simeon, and bound him before their eyes." Genesis 42:18-24.**

The brothers now accused one another in the presence of Joseph, not knowing that he understood every word. Joseph moved to tears turned away so that they might not see his tears. On regaining his composure, he now had Simeon bound before them. Simeon may have been the mastermind in the plot to murder Joseph and for this reason he may have been chosen as the hostage.

"²⁵ Then Joseph commanded to fill their sacks with corn, and to restore every man's money into his sack, and to give them provision for the way: and thus did he unto them.²⁶ And they laded their asses with the corn, and departed thence.²⁷ And as one of them opened his sack to give his ass provender in the inn, he espied his money; for, behold, it was in his sack's mouth.²⁸ And he said unto his brethren, My money is restored; and, lo, it is even in my sack: and their heart failed them, and they were afraid, saying one to another, What is this that God hath done unto us? ²⁹ And they came unto Jacob their father unto the land of Canaan, and told him all that befell unto them…" Genesis 42:25-29.

On the road home one of the brothers opened his sack of grain to feed his donkey only to find the money used to purchase the grain had been returned. Each brother in turn checked their bags to find the same result. This they interpreted as a troubling sign. On returning home to their father they related the events of their mission and the request to bring Benjamin back with them to Egypt.

"³⁶ And Jacob their father said unto them, Me have ye bereaved of my children: Joseph is not, and Simeon is not, and ye will take Benjamin away: all these things are against me.³⁷ And Reuben spake unto his father, saying, Slay my two sons, if I bring him not to thee: deliver him into my hand, and I will bring him to thee again.³⁸ And he said, My son shall not go down with you; for his

brother is dead, and he is left alone: if mischief befall him by the way in the which ye go, then shall ye bring down my gray hairs with sorrow to the grave." Genesis 42:36-38.

Reuben's offer to return Benjamin was impulsive for he was in no position to ensure the safe return of his brother. This matter should have been brought before the Lord, but Jacob trusted in self and delayed the decision until famine almost consumed them.

The Second Mission to Egypt

"[1] And the famine was sore in the land.[2] And it came to pass, when they had eaten up the corn which they had brought out of Egypt, their father said unto them, Go again, buy us a little food.[3] And Judah spake unto him, saying, The man did solemnly protest unto us, saying, Ye shall not see my face, except your brother be with you.[4] If thou wilt send our brother with us, we will go down and buy thee food: [5] But if thou wilt not send him, we will not go down: for the man said unto us, Ye shall not see my face, except your brother be with you…" Genesis 43:1-5.

"[11] And their father Israel said unto them, If it must be so now, do this; take of the best fruits in the land in your vessels, and carry down the man a present, a little balm, and a little honey, spices, and myrrh, nuts, and almonds:[12] And take double money in your hand; and the money that was brought again in the mouth of your sacks, carry it again in your hand; peradventure it was an oversight:[13] Take also your brother, and arise, go again unto the man:[14] And God Almighty give you mercy before the man, that he may send away your other brother, and Benjamin. If I be bereaved of my children, I am bereaved." Genesis 43:11-14

"[15] And the men took that present, and they took double money in their hand and Benjamin; and rose up, and went down to Egypt, and stood before Joseph. [16] And when Joseph saw Benjamin with them, he said to the ruler of his house, Bring these men home, and slay, and make ready; for these men shall dine with me at noon.[17] And the man did as Joseph bade; and the man brought the men into Joseph's house.[18] And the men were afraid, because they were brought into Joseph's house; and they said, Because of the money that was returned in our sacks at the first time are we brought in; that he may seek occasion against us, and fall upon us, and take us for bondmen, and our asses." Genesis 43:15-18

"[19] And they came near to the steward of Joseph's house, and they communed with him at the door of the house,[20] And said, O sir, we came indeed down at the first time to buy food:[21] And it came to pass, when we came to the inn, that we opened our sacks, and, behold, every man's money was in the mouth of his sack, our money in full weight: and we have brought it again in our hand.[22] And other money have we brought down in our hands to buy food: we cannot tell who put our money in our sacks. [23] And he said, Peace be to you, fear not: your God, and the God of your father, hath given you treasure in your sacks: I had your money. And he brought Simeon out unto them." Genesis 43: 19-23.

"²⁴ And the man brought the men into Joseph's house, and gave them water, and they washed their feet; and he gave their asses provender.²⁵ And they made ready the present against Joseph came at noon: for they heard that they should eat bread there.²⁶ And when Joseph came home, they brought him the present which was in their hand into the house, and bowed themselves to him to the earth.

²⁷ And he asked them of their welfare, and said, Is your father well, the old man of whom ye spake? Is he yet alive?²⁸ And they answered, Thy servant our father is in good health, he is yet alive. And they bowed down their heads, and made obeisance.²⁹ And he lifted up his eyes, and saw his brother Benjamin, his mother's son, and said, Is this your younger brother, of whom ye spake unto me? And he said, God be gracious unto thee, my son." Genesis 43:24-29.

"³⁰ And Joseph made haste; for his bowels did yearn upon his brother: and he sought where to weep; and he entered into his chamber, and wept there.³¹ And he washed his face, and went out, and refrained himself, and said, Set on bread.³² And they set on for him by himself, and for them by themselves, and for the Egyptians, which did eat with him, by themselves: because the Egyptians might not eat bread with the Hebrews; for that is an abomination unto the Egyptians.

³³ And they sat before him, the firstborn according to his birthright, and the youngest according to his youth: and the men marvelled one at another.³⁴ And he took and sent messes unto them from before him: but Benjamin's mess was five times so much as any of theirs.

And they drank, and were merry with him." Genesis 43:30-34.

Joseph now sat at a table set apart from his brothers on account of his high rank. The brothers were amazed that they were seated according to their ages, from the oldest to the youngest. Joseph accordingly sent from his table to their table portions of food, Benjamin who was the guest of honor received portions five times that of his brothers. Joseph desired to see their attitude toward their youngest brother, were they still callous and conniving or had they been sanctified through the years and through the circumstances of life? Despite this small test the scriptures declared they enjoyed one another's company.

CHAPTER 35

JOSEPH REVEALS HIS IDENTITY

Joseph's Administers His Final Test

"[1] And he commanded the steward of his house, saying, Fill the men's sacks with food, as much as they can carry, and put every man's money in his sack's mouth.[2] And put my cup, the silver cup, in the sack's mouth of the youngest, and his corn money. And he did according to the word that Joseph had spoken.[3] As soon as the morning was light, the men were sent away, they and their asses.

[4] And when they were gone out of the city, and not yet far off, Joseph said unto his steward, Up, follow after the men; and when thou dost overtake them, say unto them, Wherefore have ye rewarded evil for good? [5] Is not this it in which my lord drinketh, and whereby indeed he divineth? ye have done evil in so doing." Genesis 44:1-5.

Joseph now plants a silver cup in Benjamin's bag and then has his servants overtake the Hebrew company on their way home accusing them of theft. Joseph wanted to create a situation in which he could claim Benjamin as his servant so that he might see what his brothers would do.

Would they simply accept the decision and return to Canaan with the heartbreaking news or would they do everything in their power to prevent this from happening. Thus, he would determine their true feelings both toward their father and their youngest brother. Were they willing to sacrifice self that their father's feelings might be spared the loss of another son or would they care less. Jacob provided them with an easy way to dispose of their brother if they would so choose.

"⁶ And he overtook them, and he spake unto them these same words.⁷ And they said unto him, Wherefore saith my lord these words? God forbid that thy servants should do according to this thing: ⁸ Behold, the money, which we found in our sacks' mouths, we brought again unto thee out of the land of Canaan: how then should we steal out of thy lord's house silver or gold? ⁹ With whomsoever of thy servants it be found, both let him die, and we also will be my lord's bondmen. ¹⁰ And he said, Now also let it be according unto your words: he with whom it is found shall be my servant; and ye shall be blameless.

¹¹ Then they speedily took down every man his sack to the ground, and opened every man his sack.¹² And he searched, and began at the eldest, and left at the youngest: and the cup was found in Benjamin's sack.¹³ Then they rent their clothes, and laded every man his ass, and returned to the city.

¹⁴ And Judah and his brethren came to Joseph's house; for he was yet there: and they fell before him on the ground.¹⁵ And Joseph said unto them, What deed is this that ye have done? wot ye not that such a man as I can certainly divine? ¹⁶ And Judah said, What shall we say unto my lord? what shall we speak? or how shall we clear ourselves? God hath found out the iniquity of thy servants: behold, we are my lord's servants, both we, and he also with whom the cup is found.¹⁷ And he said, God forbid that I should do so: but the man in whose hand the cup is found, he shall be my servant; and as for

you, get you up in peace unto your father.

[18] Then Judah came near unto him, and said, Oh my lord, let thy servant, I pray thee, speak a word in my lord's ears, and let not thine anger burn against thy servant: for thou art even as Pharaoh.[19] My lord asked his servants, saying, Have ye a father, or a brother? [20] And we said unto my lord, We have a father, an old man, and a child of his old age, a little one; and his brother is dead, and he alone is left of his mother, and his father loveth him.[21] And thou saidst unto thy servants, Bring him down unto me, that I may set mine eyes upon him.[22] And we said unto my lord, The lad cannot leave his father: for if he should leave his father, his father would die.

[23] And thou saidst unto thy servants, Except your youngest brother come down with you, ye shall see my face no more.[24] And it came to pass when we came up unto thy servant my father, we told him the words of my lord.[25] And our father said, Go again, and buy us a little food.[26] And we said, We cannot go down: if our youngest brother be with us, then will we go down: for we may not see the man's face, except our youngest brother be with us.

[27] And thy servant my father said unto us, Ye know that my wife bare me two sons: [28] And the one went out from me, and I said, Surely he is torn in pieces; and I saw him not since:[29] And if ye take this also from me, and mischief befall him, ye shall bring down my gray hairs with sorrow to the grave.[30] Now therefore when I come to thy servant my father, and the lad be not with us; seeing that his life is bound up in the lad's life;[31] It

shall come to pass, when he seeth that the lad is not with us, that he will die: and thy servants shall bring down the gray hairs of thy servant our father with sorrow to the grave.

[32] For thy servant became surety for the lad unto my father, saying, If I bring him not unto thee, then I shall bear the blame to my father for ever.[33] Now therefore, I pray thee, let thy servant abide instead of the lad a bondman to my lord; and let the lad go up with his brethren.[34] For how shall I go up to my father, and the lad be not with me? lest peradventure I see the evil that shall come on my father." Genesis 44:6-34.

Judah now approaches Joseph as the governor and pledges himself as a slave instead of Benjamin. Judah's tender appeal demonstrated his loving affection toward his aged father and toward his brother Benjamin, a marked contrast to years before when he plotted with his brothers to murder and then later sell Joseph into Egypt.

Joseph Reveals Himself

"[1] Then Joseph could not refrain himself before all them that stood by him; and he cried, Cause every man to go out from me. And there stood no man with him, while Joseph made himself known unto his brethren.[2] And he wept aloud: and the Egyptians and the house of Pharaoh heard.

[3] And Joseph said unto his brethren, I am Joseph; doth my father yet live? And his brethren could not answer him; for they were troubled at his presence.[4] And Joseph said unto his brethren, Come near to me, I pray you. And they came near. And he said, I am Joseph

your brother, whom ye sold into Egypt." Genesis 45:1-4.

The brothers had now given ample evidence of the sanctification that had taken place in their hearts. Sending the servants from the room, he now made himself known to them as their brother. Joseph's house was so close to the palace that even the household of Pharaoh heard his wailing. Joseph no longer spoke through an interpreter but spoke to them in their own language.

Could it be that the one whom they sold into slavery was now the governor of Egypt second only to Pharaoh himself? Joseph now asks about his father; he had been told several times in previous interviews that his father was yet alive but now he asks again because his heart was yearning to hear more about his beloved father.

"⁵ Now therefore be not grieved, nor angry with yourselves, that ye sold me hither: for God did send me before you to preserve life.⁶ For these two years hath the famine been in the land: and yet there are five years, in the which there shall neither be earing nor harvest.⁷ And God sent me before you to preserve you a posterity in the earth, and to save your lives by a great deliverance.⁸ So now it was not you that sent me hither, but God: and he hath made me a father to Pharaoh, and lord of all his house, and a ruler throughout all the land of Egypt." Genesis 45:5-8.

Joseph now in love assures them that he had no intention of harming them and that his sale into Egypt was within the providences of God. Through this experience Joseph went from being a spoiled son, to become a slave, then a prisoner and finally the ruler of Egypt. In all this the hand of God could be seen. Through this experience Joseph and his family were both sanctified and their lives were preserved so that the promise made to Abraham so many years before would be fulfilled. So many of life's bitter trials are overruled by a loving Father that we might be made selfless.

"⁹ Haste ye, and go up to my father, and say unto him, Thus saith thy son Joseph, God hath made me lord of all Egypt: come down unto me, tarry not: ¹⁰ And thou shalt dwell in the land of Goshen, and thou shalt be near unto me, thou, and thy children, and thy children's children, and thy flocks, and thy herds, and all that thou hast:¹¹ And there will I nourish thee; for yet there are five years of famine; lest thou, and thy household, and all that thou hast, come to poverty.

¹² And, behold, your eyes see, and the eyes of my brother Benjamin, that it is my mouth that speaketh unto you.¹³ And ye shall tell my father of all my glory in Egypt, and of all that ye have seen; and ye shall haste and bring down my father hither.¹⁴ And he fell upon his brother Benjamin's neck, and wept; and Benjamin wept upon his neck.¹⁵ Moreover he kissed all his brethren, and wept upon them: and after that his brethren talked with him.

¹⁶ And the fame thereof was heard in Pharaoh's house, saying, Joseph's brethren are come: and it pleased Pharaoh well, and his servants.¹⁷ And Pharaoh said unto Joseph, Say unto thy brethren, This do ye; lade your beasts, and go, get you unto the land of Canaan; ¹⁸ And take your father and your households, and come unto me: and I will give you the good of the land of Egypt, and ye shall eat the fat of the land.

[19] Now thou art commanded, this do ye; take you wagons out of the land of Egypt for your little ones, and for your wives, and bring your father, and come.[20] Also regard not your stuff; for the good of all the land of Egypt is yours.[21] And the children of Israel did so: and Joseph gave them wagons, according to the commandment of Pharaoh, and gave them provision for the way.

[22] To all of them he gave each man changes of raiment; but to Benjamin he gave three hundred pieces of silver, and five changes of raiment.[23] And to his father he sent after this manner; ten asses laden with the good things of Egypt, and ten she asses laden with corn and bread and meat for his father by the way.[24] So he sent his brethren away, and they departed: and he said unto them, See that ye fall not out by the way.[25] And they went up out of Egypt, and came into the land of Canaan unto Jacob their father,

[26] And told him, saying, Joseph is yet alive, and he is governor over all the land of Egypt. And Jacob's heart fainted, for he believed them not.[27] And they told him all the words of Joseph, which he had said unto them: and when he saw the wagons which Joseph had sent to carry him, the spirit of Jacob their father revived: [28] And Israel said, It is enough; Joseph my son is yet alive: I will go and see him before I die." Genesis 45:9-28.

CHAPTER 36

JACOB' LAST YEARS

Jacob Departs for Egypt

"**¹ And Israel took his journey with all that he had, and came to Beersheba, and offered sacrifices unto the God of his father Isaac. ² And God spake unto Israel in the visions of the night, and said, Jacob, Jacob. And he said, Here am I.³ And he said, I am God, the God of thy father: fear not to go down into Egypt; for I will there make of thee a great nation: ⁴ I will go down with thee into Egypt; and I will also surely bring thee up again: and Joseph shall put his hand upon thine eyes." Genesis 46:1-4.**

Joseph had called for his father, but Jacob waited for divine approval, which had been granted to him in a dream with the promise to restore them again to the Land of Promise. The company that went down into Egypt is detailed in Genesis 46:8-27. The list does not include his sons' wives, or their married daughters or their families.

Jacobs Posterity	
	Number
Jacobs 11 sons & 1 unmarried daughter	12
Reuben's sons	4
Simeon's sons	6
Levi's sons	3
Judah's 3 sons and two grandsons	5
Issachar's sons	4
Zebulun's sons	4
Gad's sons	7
Asher's 4 sons, 1 daughter, 2 grandsons	7
Dan's son	1
Naphtali's sons	4
Benjamin's sons	10
Total	**66**
Grand Total: (+Jacob, Joseph & his 2 sons)	**70**

"**28** **And he sent Judah before him unto Joseph, to direct his face unto Goshen; and they came into the land of Goshen.** **29** **And Joseph made ready his chariot, and went up to meet Israel his father, to Goshen, and presented himself unto him; and he fell on his neck, and wept on his neck a good while.** **30** **And Israel said unto Joseph, Now let me die, since I have seen thy face, because thou art yet alive.**

31 **And Joseph said unto his brethren, and unto his father's house, I will go up, and shew Pharaoh, and say unto him, My brethren, and my father's house, which were in the land of Canaan, are come unto me;** **32** **And the men are shepherds, for their trade hath been to feed cattle; and they have brought their flocks, and their**

herds, and all that they have.

^{33} And it shall come to pass, when Pharaoh shall call you, and shall say, What is your occupation?^{34} That ye shall say, Thy servants' trade hath been about cattle from our youth even until now, both we, and also our fathers: that ye may dwell in the land of Goshen; for every shepherd is an abomination unto the Egyptians." Genesis 46:28-34

The meeting between father and son separated by 22 years of supposed death, the expression of love and tears is now only the subject of the imagination. Joseph instructed his brothers if asked of their occupation that they were to say they were shepherds thus disqualifying them from the duties of court life. The land of Goshen in the lush eastern Nile delta was subsequently given to them for farming and where they could be separate from the world.

"^{7} And Joseph brought in Jacob his father, and set him before Pharaoh: and Jacob blessed Pharaoh. ^{8} And Pharaoh said unto Jacob, How old art thou? ^{9} And Jacob said unto Pharaoh, The days of the years of my pilgrimage are an hundred and thirty years: few and evil have the days of the years of my life been, and have not attained unto the days of the years of the life of my fathers in the days of their pilgrimage. ^{10} And Jacob blessed Pharaoh, and went out from before Pharaoh.

^{11} And Joseph placed his father and his brethren, and gave them a possession in the land of Egypt, in the best of the land, in the land of Rameses, as Pharaoh had commanded. ^{12} And Joseph nourished his father, and his brethren, and all his father's household, with bread,

**according to their families... ²⁷ And Israel dwelt in the
land of Egypt, in the country of Goshen; and they had
possessions therein, and grew, and multiplied
exceedingly. ²⁸ And Jacob lived in the land of Egypt
seventeen years: so the whole age of Jacob was an
hundred forty and seven years." Genesis 47:7-12, 27, 28.**

Jacob was 130 years into his pilgrimage and lived
another 17 years in Egypt before he died at 147. Jacob was
a Hebrew, like Abraham "one who is passing through" a
traveler on a course to a destination but "[13] These all died in
faith, not having received the promises, but having seen
them afar off, and were persuaded of them, and embraced
them, and confessed that they were strangers and pilgrims
on the earth. [14] For they that say such things declare plainly
that they seek a country. [15] And truly, if they had been
mindful of that country from whence they came out, they
might have had opportunity to have returned.

[16] But now they desire a better country, that is, an
heavenly: wherefore God is not ashamed to be called their
God: for he hath prepared for them a city. [10] ... which hath
foundations, whose builder and maker is God." Hebrews 11:
13-16,10.

Jacob Adopts Joseph's Two Sons

**"[1] And it came to pass after these things, that one told
Joseph, Behold, thy father is sick: and he took with him
his two sons, Manasseh and Ephraim... ⁵ And now thy
two sons, Ephraim and Manasseh, which were born unto
thee in the land of Egypt before I came unto thee into
Egypt, are mine; as Reuben and Simeon, they shall be
mine. ⁶ And thy issue, which thou begettest after them,**

shall be thine, and shall be called after the name of their brethren in their inheritance." Genesis 48:1, 5, 6.

On hearing that his father was ill Joseph now brought his two sons, the elder Manasseh, and the younger Ephraim, to Jacob so that they might receive a blessing of the dying patriarch. Jacob interpreted the promises given at Bethel (Genesis 35:9-15) as permission to adopt the sons of Joseph and give them the same status as his own children, giving them each a portion of the inheritance.

This privilege was to be restricted to the first two sons. If any other children were to be born, they were to be included in the tribes of Manasseh and Ephraim. The adoption of his first two sons gave Joseph the portion of the birthright of the firstborn son that entitled him to double the portion of his father's inheritance.

"[8] And Israel beheld Joseph's sons, and said, Who are these? [9] And Joseph said unto his father, They are my sons, whom God hath given me in this place. And he said, Bring them, I pray thee, unto me, and I will bless them. [10] Now the eyes of Israel were dim for age, so that he could not see. And he brought them near unto him; and he kissed them, and embraced them.[11] And Israel said unto Joseph, I had not thought to see thy face: and, lo, God hath shewed me also thy seed....

[14] And Israel stretched out his right hand, and laid it upon Ephraim's head, who was the younger, and his left hand upon Manasseh's head, guiding his hands wittingly; for Manasseh was the firstborn.[15] And he blessed Joseph, and said, God, before whom my fathers Abraham and Isaac did walk, the God which fed me all

my life long unto this day," Genesis 48:8-11, 14, 15,

"^{17} And when Joseph saw that his father laid his right hand upon the head of Ephraim, it displeased him: and he held up his father's hand, to remove it from Ephraim's head unto Manasseh's head.^{18} And Joseph said unto his father, Not so, my father: for this is the firstborn; put thy right hand upon his head.^{19} And his father refused, and said, I know it, my son, I know it: he also shall become a people, and he also shall be great: but truly his younger brother shall be greater than he, and his seed shall become a multitude of nations... ^{21} And Israel said unto Joseph, Behold, I die: but God shall be with you, and bring you again unto the land of your fathers." Genesis 48:17-19, 21.

Jacob blessed the younger Ephraim with his right hand since he was to excel the older brother Manasseh. Joseph thought this was an error on account of his father's poor sight, but Jacob assured him this was intentional as led by the Holy Spirit. "^{16} The Angel which redeemed me from all evil, bless the lads;.." Genesis 48:16. Jacob asked a blessing for the boys from the "angel" with whom he wrestled and whom he acknowledged as God. While Christ had not been incarnated yet, our Savior has always been active in human history as "the angel of the Lord."

CHAPTER 37

THE TWELVE TRIBES OF ISRAEL

"[1] And Jacob called unto his sons, and said, Gather yourselves together, that I may tell you that which shall befall you in the last days. [2] Gather yourselves together, and hear, ye sons of Jacob; and hearken unto Israel your father." Genesis 49:1, 2.

Jacob now utters a blessing on each one of his sons, often termed the twelve patriarchs who were the progenitors of the twelve tribes of Israel. In these blessings Jacob outlined the characters of his sons and the future of the nation. The phrase "in the last days" simply means "in the future."

The Book of Revelation brings to view two companies of redeemed people, the "great multitude" (Revelation 7:9-14) and a group termed the "one hundred and forty-four thousand" (Revelation 7:4-8). The "great multitude" are the redeemed that come from every age since Adam while the 144,000 (12, 000 from each of the 12 tribes) are a company that have battled the mark of the beast through the ages, be it literal or spiritual Jews. This number of 144,000 is a figurative number, as God predestines no man's choice. Each of these 12 tribes will enter New Jerusalem through one of the 12 gates, 3 gates on each side of the foursquare city. (Revelation 21: 1, 10, 12-14). In numerology the number 12 indicates divine order.

Jacob had twelve sons and he adopted Joseph's two sons Manasseh and Ephraim which totals 14 Patriarchs. The descendants of Levi were not given a physical territory since they were to be the religious leaders of Israel and as such were given 48 cities scattered throughout the land. Joseph himself was not given land per say but he did receive a double portion of an inheritance through his two sons, Ephraim and Manasseh thus the sons of Jacob come to number 12 tribes in Genesis 49. In Revelation 7 the list of the twelve tribes differs; Dan and Ephraim were disinherited due to their wickedness and are thus omitted; Levi and Joseph were added back to number 12 tribes.

The history of the twelve patriarchs and their tribes is a lesson in character development. Each patriarch had defects of character, the work of self. Through the trials of life many of these men overcame their character defects. Their victories and their failures define the tribes. The men and women of spiritual Israel who make up the figurative 144,000 in part are allocated to the various tribes based on character traits not by seed affiliation as in ancient Israel.

1. Reuben

"³ Reuben, thou art my firstborn, my might, and the beginning of my strength, the excellency of dignity, and the excellency of power: ⁴ Unstable as water, thou shalt not excel; because thou wentest up to thy father's bed; then defiledst thou it: he went up to my couch." Genesis 49:3, 4.

Reuben as the firstborn son was entitled to the promises of the birthright; a double portion of his father's inheritance, the priest of the home and progenitor of the Messiah. Thus he was in the position of "excellent dignity and power." But all this was forfeited as his character was "unstable as water."

Reuben like a reed in the wind went along with his passions and lay with his father's concubine, Billah (Genesis 35:22). When his brothers plotted to kill Jospeh, Reuben protested but he did not want to displease his brothers either, so he proposed a different less evil plan by throwing him into a pit with the hope of rescuing him later. Reuben did not have the courage to stand up to his brethren, he wanted to please everyone.

As a result of his "spineless" character the birthright was divided between three of his brothers. The double portion of the father's inheritance was given to Joseph (1 Chronicles 5:1), the priesthood to Levi (Deuteronomy 33:8-11) and the lineage of the Messiah was given to Judah. (1 Chronicles 5:1, 2). The tribe of Reuben never reached any position of influence in the nation, there was no judge, no king and no prophet.

The tribe of Reuben later proved true to his brethren for after they received of their inheritance on the east side of the Jordan, they pledged to fight alongside their brethren until each tribe was given their portion of the land. (Joshua 4:12, 13). A figurative twelve thousand of the 144,000 who were "unstable as water" but have overcome their defects of character will enter the New Jerusalem under the banner of Reuben.

2. Simeon

"[5] Simeon and Levi are brethren; instruments of cruelty are in their habitations.[6] O my soul, come not thou into their secret; unto their assembly, mine honour, be not thou united: for in their anger they slew a man, and in their selfwill they digged down a wall.[7] Cursed be their anger, for it was fierce; and their wrath, for it was cruel: I will divide them in Jacob, and scatter them in Israel." Genesis 49:5, 6.

Simeon and Levi were brothers by blood but also in thoughts and actions. This is a reference to the murder of all the men of Shechem when one young man laid with Dinah their sister. Jacob predicted that the descendants of these two men would not receive their own portion of the land in Canaan but were to be scattered amongst their brethren. When the tribe of Simeon left Egypt, they were one of the strongest tribes, but by the time they entered the Promised Land they had become the weakest for many died in the desert because of their "whoredom" with the woman of Midian (Numbers 25).

Moses in his dying blessing completely passed over Simeon. The tribe received no inheritance in the land of promise except several cities scattered throughout the territory of Judah. (Joshua 19:1-9). Those who were not assimilated into the tribe of Judah migrated to areas outside of the land of promise. (1 Chronicles 4:38-43).

It may seem strange that one who was notorious for murder would have his name written on one of the gates of the New Jerusalem, but the grace of Christ is sufficient to transform the character ruined by sin. A figurative twelve thousand who have followed Satan to the depths of degradation in murder, our prisons are full of such people, will be elevated to be princes with God.

3. Levi

"5 Simeon and Levi are brethren; instruments of cruelty are in their habitations.... I will divide them in Jacob, and scatter them in Israel." Genesis 49:5, 6.

Jacob speaks of both Levi and Simeon in the same breath

since Levi was alongside Simeon in the murders of Shechem, but the tribe of Levi was able to redeem themselves by the choices they made later in life. At Mount Sinai when the people worshipped the golden calf, it was the tribe of Levi alone who remained loyal to God executing those who persisted in idolatry regardless of whether they were friends or family (Exodus 32: 27-28). As a result, the priesthood was awarded to Levi.

Since the Levites were to be the spiritual guardians of the people, they were given no land of inheritance but rather 48 cities scattered through the Promised Land so that the people would have easy access to these religious instructors (Numbers 18: 20, 21). Moses and Aaron are two of the most prominent members of the tribe of Levi. A figurative twelve thousand of the 144,000 who have demonstrated allegiance to God irrespective of family or friends will enter the New Jerusalem under the banner of Levi.

4. Judah

"[8] Judah, thou art he whom thy brethren shall praise: thy hand shall be in the neck of thine enemies; thy father's children shall bow down before thee.[9] Judah is a lion's whelp: from the prey, my son, thou art gone up: he stooped down, he couched as a lion, and as an old lion; who shall rouse him up?

[10] The sceptre shall not depart from Judah, nor a lawgiver from between his feet, until Shiloh come; and unto him shall the gathering of the people be.[11] Binding his foal unto the vine, and his ass's colt unto the choice vine; he washed his garments in wine, and his clothes in the blood of grapes: [12] His eyes shall be red with wine,

and his teeth white with milk." Genesis 49:8-12.

Judah, "The praised one," is Jacob's fourth son who received the leadership portion of the birthright forfeited by Reuben. The strength of Judah's character is compared to that of a lion. Judah was to continue as a leader amongst the tribes until Shiloh came. Shiloh means "peace giver" and refers to the Messiah who would come "binding his foal unto the vine." This was literally fulfilled when Jesus made his triumphant ride into Jerusalem riding upon a foal (Matthew 21:7).

Through highly figurative language Jacob describes the prosperity of Judah as a vine that is so strong that asses could be bound to it and the vine would be so fruitful that the juice could be used to wash one's garments and when drunk would cause the eyes and the teeth to shine.

Without the guidance of a stable home Judah got mixed up with Canaanite woman and prostitutes. Judah colluded to murder Joseph and finally was the one who proposed to sell his brother as a slave. His character, like his brethren, was molded by the jealousy of four selfish wives, but he was able to overcome these defects of character and became a leader in the family.

Jacob himself had seen these changes; Jacob rejected Reuben's offer to stand as guarantee for Benjamin's safe return, but he accepted Judah's offer. Judah's further change in character is evidenced by his eloquent selfless plea before the governor of Egypt where he offered himself as a slave instead of his brother Benjamin.

The prophet Daniel and his three companions Shadrach, Meshach and Abednego were of the tribe of Judah. Daniel was cast into the lion's den and his three companions into the fiery furnace, all coming forth unharmed. No other tribe bore more kings than Judah. King David was of the tribe of Judah and Jesus of Nazareth descended through this tribe. Jesus is the tribe's most notable character, for he is the "the Lion of the tribe of Juda, the Root of David" (Revelation 5:5). A figurative twelve thousand of the 144,000 who have overcome their selfish traits of character and have developed lion-like qualities will enter the New Jerusalem under the banner of Judah.

5. Zebulun

"[13] Zebulun shall dwell at the haven of the sea; and he shall be for an haven of ships; and his border shall be unto Zidon." Genesis 49:13.

The territory of Zebulun was located between the Mediterranean Sea and the Sea of Galilee. (Joshua 19:10-16) but its boundaries did not actually reach these bodies of water although at one time they may have since Moses in his parting blessing spoke of Zebulun as a sea-faring people (Deut. 33:18, 19).

Little is known of the character of the patriarch Zebulun whose name means, "to dwell." Jacob describes Zebulun as a "haven of the sea" indicating they were a peaceful and quiet people. As ships find safety at port, so those who come to associate with those in the tribe of Zebulun will find this similar rest in their presence. The childhood and ministry of Jesus was set predominantly in Nazareth and Galilee both within the borders of Zebulun.

During the Battle of Megiddo in the time of the Judges, Zebulun "…were a people that jeoparded their lives unto the death in the high places of the field." Judges 5:18. Furthermore they were self-sacrificing for "they took no gain of money." (Judges 5:19). It was also said that the people of Zebulun were ones "that handle the pen of the writer" (Judges 5:14). While skilled and brave in war they were also a creative and literary people.

Two hundred years later at the time when David was to be crowned king over Israel all twelve tribes were represented but no tribe excelled the tribe of Zebulun. Of Zebulun "such as went forth to battle, expert in war, with all instruments of war, fifty thousand, which could keep rank: they were not of double heart." (1 Chronicles 12:33). A figurative twelve thousand of the 144,000 who with singleness of heart and quietness of spirit utilizing their monetary and literary talents to advance the kingdom will enter the New Jerusalem under the banner of Zebulun.

6. Issachar

"**[14] Issachar is a strong ass couching down between two burdens: [15] And he saw that rest was good, and the land that it was pleasant; and bowed his shoulder to bear, and became a servant unto tribute." Genesis 49:14, 15.**

Jacob compares Issachar to a patient donkey bearing two heavy saddlebags, patient in labor and unbeatable in war. They "were valiant men of might." (1Chronicles 7:1-5). Issachar's insight and judgment was seen when it came to crowning David King over Israel, "The children of Issachar were… men that had understanding of the times, to know what Israel ought to do." (1 Chronicles 12:32). Later in the Battle of Megiddo Issachar bore the brunt of the battle, "the princes of Issachar were with Deborah; even Issachar, and also Barak" (Judges 5:15). A figurative twelve thousand of the 144,000 who with strong insight and judgment with good work ethic in the cause of God will enter the New Jerusalem under the banner of Issachar.

7. Dan

"[16] Dan shall judge his people, as one of the tribes of Israel.[17] Dan shall be a serpent by the way, an adder in the path, that biteth the horse heels, so that his rider shall fall backward." Genesis 49:16-18.**

The first part of the blessing demonstrates the character that Dan may have possessed as a Judge in Israel had he embraced selflessness but instead he is compared to a self-serving snake attacking unsuspecting travelers. Back stabbers are those who are two faced, like snakes in the grass ready to turn without a moment's notice using their tongues which is "full of deadly poison." (James 3: 6-8). "Lord, who shall abide in Thy tabernacle? who shall dwell in Thy holy hill? He that backbiteth not with his tongue, nor doeth evil to his neighbor, nor taketh up reproach against his neighbor." Psalms 15:1,3. The tribe of Dan was later responsible for introducing idol worship in Israel (Judges 18). Given his two-faced backstabbing nature Dan was disinherited and is omitted in the numeration of the tribes of Revelation Chapter 7. The most prominent member of this tribe was the judge Samson who judged Israel for 20 years.

8. Gad

"Gad, a troop shall overcome him: but he shall overcome at the last." Genesis 49: 19.

The Gadites were "men of might, and men of war fit for the battle, that could handle shield and buckler, whose faces were like the faces of lions, and were as swift as the roes upon the mountains" 1 Chronicles 12:8. The Gadites were brave and ferocious as lions but agile as deer ("roes") in warfare.

The most prominent member of this tribe was the prophet Elijah who called Israel and King Ahab to repentance. Elijah was one of but 7000 in Israel who would not bow the knee to the sun god Baal. Elijah challenged the priest of Baal to a dual sacrifice to see who was God? - Yahweh or Baal. Fire came from heaven consuming Elijah's sacrifice and the stone altar itself.

Elijah ascended to heaven without seeing death and together with Moses met with Jesus on the Mount of Olives to strengthen Him in the path to Calvary (Luke 9: 28-31). A figurative twelve thousand of the 144,000 who have stood against the gods of self-serving will enter the New Jerusalem under the banner of Gad.

9. Asher

"Out of Asher his bread shall be fat, and he shall yield royal dainties." Genesis 49:20. Genesis 30:13.

These words indicate that the tribe of Asher would be a prosperous people. The tribe received of the lowlands of Carmel on the Mediterranean, one of the most fertile portions blessed with a wealth of oil and wheat. The name

"Asher" in Hebrew means "happy."

The later benediction of Moses declared; "Let Asher be blessed with children; let him be acceptable to his brethren, and let him dip his foot in oil. Thy shoes shall be iron and brass; and as thy days, so shall thy strength be." Deuteronomy 33: 24, 25.

Asher and his descendants had developed a character resilient to trials of life as though their oiled feet were shoed with brass. They had developed the emotional reserves to deal with hardship, they were happy, blessed and complained not. A Figurative twelve thousand of the 144,000 who have overcome their defects of character will enter the New Jerusalem under the banner of Asher.

10. Naphtali

"[21] Naphtali is a hind let loose: he giveth goodly words." Genesis 49:21.

A hind, a female deer, is a meek animal; those of the tribe were meek as was shown in their "goodly words," words to encourage the broken hearted. "Pleasant words are as a honeycomb, sweet to the soul, and health to the bones." Proverbs 16:24.

"Blessed are the meek: for they shall inherit the earth" Matthew 5:5. Meekness, quietness of spirit, is not pretentious as it is rooted in selflessness. Meekness does not provoke arguments, nor does it answer back angrily but soothes irritated feelings. Meekness is "even the ornament of a meek and quiet spirit, which is in the sight of God of great price." 1 Peter 3:4. Moses in his departing blessing

259

declared, "O Naphtali, satisfied with favour, and full with the blessing of the Lord." Deuteronomy 33: 23.

In the Battle of Megiddo, "Zebulun and Naphtali were a people that jeoparded their lives unto the death in the high places of the field." Judges 5:18. The men of Naphtali and Zebulun were determined to conquer or be killed, for them the truth of God was more important than life itself. A Figurative twelve thousand of the 144,000 who have overcome their defective characters, bearing hardship with meekness and "goodly words," will be found worthy to enter the New Jerusalem under the banner of Naphtali.

11. Joseph

"**22 Joseph is a fruitful bough, even a fruitful bough by a well; whose branches run over the wall: 23 The archers have sorely grieved him, and shot at him, and hated him:24 But his bow abode in strength, and the arms of his hands were made strong by the hands of the mighty God of Jacob; (from thence is the shepherd, the stone of Israel:)25 Even by the God of thy father, who shall help thee; and by the Almighty, who shall bless thee with blessings of heaven above, blessings of the deep that lieth under, blessings of the breasts, and of the womb:**

26 The blessings of thy father have prevailed above the blessings of my progenitors unto the utmost bound of the everlasting hills: they shall be on the head of Joseph, and on the crown of the head of him that was separate from his brethren." Genesis 49:22-26.

Jacob now compares the character of Joseph to that of a fruitful vine. Before being sold into Egypt Joseph was spoiled through favoritism but God used his slavery and imprisonment to refine his character. Through his dealing with his brothers, we see no revenge but only a spirit of love and forgiveness. The virtues of his character are as refreshing to a traveler who passing through a dry land finds relief from the fruit of a tree hanging over a wall. Joseph's life demonstrated fruit that is of heavenly origin and in this he is presented as a tree planted on the other side of the wall next to the well.

As a slave Joseph was faithful in every duty from the smallest to the greatest. By being faithful in little things, we can be trusted to be faithful with much. A figurative twelve thousand of the 144,000 who were once spoiled children and have overcome their character defects of self, willing rather to die than sin against God will enter the New Jerusalem under the banner of Joseph.

12. Benjamin

"²⁷ Benjamin shall ravin as a wolf: in the morning he shall devour the prey, and at night he shall divide the spoil." Genesis 49:27.

Jacob describes a child who was raised without parental restraint and who would become oppositional, angry, and resentful when corrected or redirected. Since his mother had died in childbirth Jacob undoubtedly overcompensated by loose and permissive parenting until the will of the child, like a wolf, had become the law of the house. His combative nature was expressed through his descendants who made war against the other tribes (Judges 20:21).

The tribe of Benjamin was skilled in war, they could "sling stones at a hair breadth, and not miss." Judges 20: 16. They "could use both the right hand and the left in hurling stones and shooting arrows out of a bow." 1 Chronicles 12: 1, 2. The benediction of Moses however predicted a change in character, and of Benjamin he said: "The beloved of the Lord shall dwell in safety by him; and the Lord shall cover him all the day long, and he shall dwell between His shoulders." (Deut. 33:12).

The apostle Paul is the tribe's most notable character. Paul before his conversion was the fiercest persecutor of the early church and many martyrs died at his hand. But under the converting power of the Holy Spirits his wolf-like character was changed from a persecutor to one who became a missionary. Paul traveled all over Palestine and Asia spreading the words of the gospel. A figurative twelve thousand of the 144,000 who were once like ravenous wolves but who have come under the molding power of the Holy Spirit will enter the New Jerusalem under the banner of Benjamin.

13. Ephraim

"[14] **And Israel stretched out his right hand, and laid it upon Ephraim's head, who was the younger, and his left hand upon Manasseh's head, guiding his hands wittingly; for Manasseh was the firstborn.[15] And he blessed Joseph, and said, God, before whom my fathers Abraham and Isaac did walk, the God which fed me all my life long unto this day, [16] The Angel which redeemed me from all evil, bless the lads; and let my name be named on them, and the name of my fathers Abraham and Isaac; and let them grow into a multitude in the midst of the earth." 48:14-16.**

By divine inspiration Jacob had deliberately placed his right hand on the youngest for he would excel his older brother in numbers. At the time of Moses, Manasseh numbered 20,000 more than did Ephraim (Numbers 26:34,37), however the prophecy of Jacob met its fulfillment after the time of the judges when Ephraim had so increased in size that it took the leadership of the northern ten tribes. The tribe of Ephraim, however, became fully devoted to idolatry after they settled in the land of Canaan and were eventually carried captive into Assyria. By their choice they were disinherited from their heavenly inheritance, no gate or tribe will be found in the New Jerusalem.

14. Manasseh

Manasseh, the oldest son of Joseph, at the time of settlement in the land of Canaan was greater than Ephraim but by the time of the judges Manasseh decreased in size while his younger brother rapidly increased and surpassed him in numbers. When David's family was captured, men from the tribe of Manasseh came to his assistance. The people of Manasseh participated in the reforms instituted in the land under the kings Asa, Hezekiah and Josiah. Gideon is the tribe's most prominent character. A figurative twelve thousand of the 144,000 will enter the New Jerusalem under the banner of Manasseh.

THE TWELVE TRIBES
OF ISRAEL
Around 1200-1050 B.C.
(according to the Book of Joshua)

Sidon

ARAMEANS

Tyre
Ijon
Dan

ASHER
NAPHTALI
Kedesh

Mediterranean
Sea

Hazor

Chinnereth

Ashteroth

Achshaph
Hamath
BASAN

Helkath
Mount Tabor
ZEBULUN
Jokneam
ISSACHAR
Camon
Edrei

Dor
Japhia

Megiddo
Jezreel

Taanach
Bethshean
Ramoth-Gilead

MANASSEH

Tirzah

Shamir
Zaphon

Shechem
Mahanaim

Pirathon

Gathrimmon
Aphek
Shiloh

Joppa
EPHRAIM
GAD
AMMON

DAN
Bethel
Jazer
Rabbath Ammon

Eltekeh
Bethoron
Ai
Gilgal

Gezer
Gibeon
Jericho

Gibbethon
BENJAMIN
Heshbon
Mephaath

Ashdod
Ekron

Ashkelon
Gath
Jarmuth
Jerusalem
Bezer
Mount Nebo

Bethlehem
REUBEN

PHILISTIA
Lachish
JUDAH
Jahaza

Gaza
Hebron

Debir
Eshtemoa

Gerar
Arad

Beersheba
MOAB

SIMEON
Kirhareseth

AMALEK
Zoar

Wilderness of
Zin
EDOM

Tamar Zalmona

Bozrah

Kadesh
Punon

CHAPTER 38

THE END OF THE PATRIARCHAL PERIOD

The Death of Jacob

"[28] All these are the twelve tribes of Israel: and this is it that their father spake unto them, and blessed them; every one according to his blessing he blessed them. [29] And he charged them, and said unto them, I am to be gathered unto my people: bury me with my fathers ... [33] And when Jacob had made an end of commanding his sons, he gathered up his feet into the bed, and yielded up the ghost, and was gathered unto his people." Genesis 49:28, 29, 33.

"[1] And Joseph fell upon his father's face, and wept upon him, and kissed him. [2] And Joseph commanded his servants the physicians to embalm his father: and the physicians embalmed Israel. [3] And forty days were fulfilled for him; for so are fulfilled the days of those which are embalmed: and the Egyptians mourned for him threescore and ten days.

[4] And when the days of his mourning were past, Joseph spake unto the house of Pharaoh, saying, If now I have found grace in your eyes, speak, I pray you, in the ears of Pharaoh, saying, [5] My father made me swear, saying, Lo, I die: in my grave which I have digged for me in the land of Canaan, there shalt thou bury me. Now therefore let me go up, I pray thee, and bury my father, and I will come again. [6] And Pharaoh said, Go up, and bury thy father, according as he made thee swear." Genesis 50: 1-6

The Death of Joseph

"²² And Joseph dwelt in Egypt, he, and his father's house: and Joseph lived an hundred and ten years.²³ And Joseph saw Ephraim's children of the third generation: the children also of Machir the son of Manasseh were brought up upon Joseph's knees.

²⁴ And Joseph said unto his brethren, I die: and God will surely visit you, and bring you out of this land unto the land which he sware to Abraham, to Isaac, and to Jacob.²⁵ And Joseph took an oath of the children of Israel, saying, God will surely visit you, and ye shall carry up my bones from hence.²⁶ So Joseph died, being an hundred and ten years old: and they embalmed him, and he was put in a coffin in Egypt." Genesis 50:22-26.

Since Joseph had been born when his father was 91, he was therefore 56 years old at his father's death and he outlived his father by another 54 years dying at the age of 110.

Joseph requested that when they should leave Egypt that his bones be carried to the Land of Promise. By this act of faith, the patriarchal period comes to an end. The temporary tomb of Joseph in Egypt was a constant reminder to the Hebrews that their permanent home would be in the land of Canaan. The hour of their slavery was approaching but not all the power of Pharaoh could frustrate the purposes of heaven, for at the time appointed, the people were liberated on eagle's wings by the mighty hand of a loving Father.

Printed in the USA
CPSIA information can be obtained
at www.ICGtesting.com
LVHW051918210924
791652LV00019B/274